UP TOP

Up Top

From Lunatic Asylum to Community Care
A Century of the Mid Wales Mental Hospital

Hugh Purcell
with Margaret Percy

First impression: 2018

© Copyright Hugh Purcell and Y Lolfa Cyf., 2018

Cover photograph: Margaret Percy
Cover design: Ceri Jones

ISBN: 978 1 78461 591 8

Published and printed in Wales
on paper from well-maintained forests by
Y Lolfa Cyf., Talybont, Ceredigion SY24 5HE
website www.ylolfa.com
e-mail ylolfa@ylolfa.com
tel 01970 832 304
fax 832 782

Contents

Introduction: The Mad Woman   7

Chapter One: Life in the Asylum   13
   The new asylum   13
   Laws for lunatics   19
   The patients   27
   The attendants   34
   The treatment   45
   'Shell-shock' victims of the Great War   49
   From asylum to mental hospital   52
   The spectre of schizophrenia   56

Chapter Two: Camp 234   59
   Talgarth Military Hospital 1940–1947   59
   Camp 234   69
   The truth about Rudolph Hess   82
   The strange case of Arnold Buchthal   86
   The soldiers left behind   87
   The civilian hospital 1940–1947   90

Chapter Three: O, Brave New World!   95
   Frontal leucotomy   98
   Electroconvulsive therapy (ECT)   103
   Deep sleep treatment   110
   The chemical revolution   112
   Life on the wards   118
   Outpatients   126
   The winds of change   129
   The Mental Health Act of 1959   130

Chapter Four: In-Care, Out-Care   **135**

    Into the community   137

    Institutionalisation   138

    Opening the doors   144

    The long-stay wards   147

    Outings   153

    Wards 7 and 8   156

    Behavioural therapy   164

    Psychotherapy   169

    Occupational therapy   172

    The Powys School of Nursing   175

Chapter Five: Closure   **177**

    Countdown   180

    Zero   185

    Those shuffling feet from the past   192

Acknowledgements   **194**

Index   **196**

The Mad Woman

'You've read *Kilvert's Diary*, haven't you?' asked retired school teacher Gaynor Davies when I met her in Talgarth. She was referring to the well-known diary of Francis Kilvert, who was curate to the vicar of Clyro between 1865 and 1872. His descriptions of life in the border country have become a minor classic, published and reprinted many times. 'Do you remember his visit to the mad woman?' Gaynor went on. How could I forget it?

Thursday, September Eve, 1871
I went up to Lower Cwmgwanon to see the old mad woman Mrs Watkins. Her son was out in the harvest field carrying oats, and I had to wait till he came in to go upstairs with me.

While I waited in the kitchen the low deep voice upstairs began calling, 'Murder! John Lloyd! John Lloyd! Murder!'

He led the way up the broad oak staircase into a fetid room, darkened. The window was blocked up with stools and chairs to prevent the poor mad creature from throwing herself out. She had broken all the window glass and all the crockery. There was nothing in her room but her bed and chair. She lay with the blanket over her head. When her son turned the blanket down I was almost frightened. It was a mad skeleton with such a wild scared animal's face as I never saw before. Her dark hair was tossed weird and unkempt, and she stared at me like a wild beast.

But she began directly to talk rationally, though her mind wandered at moments. I repeated the Lord's Prayer and the old familiar words seemed to come back to her by degrees, till she could say it alone.

When I went away she besought me earnestly to come again. 'You'll promise to come again now. You'll promise', she said eagerly.

'Her family would have been so relieved if the asylum had been open then' said Gaynor, and how right she was, but no doubt poor Mrs Watkins was long dead before the Brecknock and Radnor Joint Asylum at Talgarth opened in February 1903.

At the opening ceremony, Lord Glanusk, Chairman of the Joint Committee, announced with pride: 'Everything has been done that human ingenuity could devise for the happiness and safety of the inmates, and under the blessing of God, for their speedy restoration to health'. He spoke with the confidence of the Edwardian era, and according to the standards of that age he was right. Considering the desperate extremes of mental illness and the incurability of what was then called 'congenital insanity' (meaning 'idiocy' and 'imbecility'), a surprising number of short-stay 'inmates' were discharged as 'recovered' or at least 'relieved', and the growing number of long-stay patients were cared for with kindness.

Now the asylum has gone, but its ghosts remain. Long since renamed the Mid Wales Hospital, it closed in 2000 and in the intervening years a planning impasse has allowed the historic site above the town to decline into a vast and hideous semi-ruin. Until very recently, seekers of the paranormal – 'How many spirits are there here? Don't be shy! Come and talk to us' – roamed the rubble-strewn corridors at night; trophy hunters walked off with possible museum pieces like restraint and resuscitation equipment used in ECT (electro-convulsive therapy). Graffiti in Spanish reveals that migrants have dossed down here; and splats of exploded paint balls suggest wild games have taken place. The 1970s Treatment Centre is piled with medical jumble, including a dentist's chair; its walls are decorated with Walt Disney caricatures, including a sinister Mickey Mouse.

On the Mid Wales Hospital website is a film that intercuts photos of the vandalised ruins of today with pictures of the asylum at its opening in 1903. The proud Edwardian patriarchs sit outside its entrance. Behind them is the typical Victorian asylum that Enoch Powell described in a seminal speech he made in 1961 when he was Minister of Health: 'There they stand, isolated, majestic, imperious… the asylums our forefathers built with such immense solidity to express the notions of the day'. The film is set to a Welsh choir singing 'Myfanwy', which adds to the overwhelming melancholy.

Researching the history of 'up top', as the Mid Wales Hospital was referred to in Talgarth – and what a double meaning that has! – leaves haunting memories. One I can't get out of my mind was put there by Gaynor Davies. She told me that in the 1940s she was a child living on a farm near the remote church of St Ellyw at Llanelieu. Every month or so on a Sunday a party of patients from the Mid Wales was escorted across the fields for their own church service. They shambled along, some waving their arms and shouting; they carried red and white paper flowers presumably made in occupational therapy. After the service they came to Gaynor's farm and her mother made them tea. Before they walked back across the fields they presented her with the bouquet of paper flowers.

To a social historian like myself, the derelict buildings of the Mid Wales Hospital are an irresistible, if sinister, attraction. On these wards for a hundred years lived and died – to use the changing language of the century – hundreds of lunatics, imbeciles, manic depressives, mental defectives, shell-shocked soldiers, schizophrenics, EMIs (Elderly Mentally Ill) and the lesser-abled ill of our society. The Mid Wales was a total institution, an enclosed community that enveloped people's lives. This applies to the staff too: Talgarth born and bred, some working at the Mid Wales through three generations, many of them serving 'up top' from first pay packet to retirement. What care and treatment were the patients given? What was the relationship between patients and staff? How did the Mid Wales shape their lives?

In the autumn of 2016 the Wellcome Collection in London presented an exhibition, *Bedlam, the asylum and beyond*. Coinciding with the topical interest in mental illness, it offered a multi-media demonstration of what it means to be 'mad'. For anybody with introspection and empathy it must have been unsettling; for me, it certainly was. Where is the boundary between sanity and insanity? Even, at times, am I crossing this boundary? Am I 'losing my mind'?

The exhibition showed how mental illness has been treated over the last century. The asylums believed in fresh air, exercise and hot baths. Next, the mental hospitals experimented with boring holes in heads, electrocuting minds and sending patients into weeks of 'deep sleep'. The psychiatric hospitals took over with ever-refining forms of therapy: behaviour therapy, psychotherapy, psychoanalysis, and now cognitive behavioural therapy (CBT). Over the last half century an ongoing chemical revolution has produced more and more beneficial drugs – at a cost. All these treatments were provided at the Mid Wales.

My two visits to *Bedlam, the asylum and beyond* made a deep impression on me. Then, of course, the Mid Wales was on my doorstep and nobody had told its history. For a social historian that offered a unique opportunity. Living in the environs of Talgarth are any number of retired staff from the Mid Wales, mostly former nurses, all of whom have vivid memories and enduring loyalty to the Hospital. I thank them all, by name, below.

There are written archives, too. The Brecon and Radnor Joint Counties Asylum, to which Montgomeryshire was soon added, was nothing if not rigorous in keeping its written and photographic records and these are available in the Powys County Archive at Llandrindod Wells. I am very grateful to the Library for allowing me to use personal records with photographs of patients who were in the asylum more than a hundred years ago, provided that I did not identify them by name.

At the National Archives at Kew in London are stored the General Nursing Council Reports on the Mid Wales between 1947 and 1971, and also the weekly War Diary (so called) of Lt Col. Peter Drummond, Medical Superintendent of the Mid Wales when it became Talgarth Military Hospital during the last war. I spent one week researching these.

A unique record of Camp 234, that is the POW contingent at Talgarth Military Hospital, is stored in the Rare Documents Collection at the Wellcome Collection Library. This is the war diary left by Dr Hugo Rast, the President of the Mixed Medical Commission that was charged with recommending to the War Office the names of mentally ill POWs from Germany and Italy at Camp 234 who should be repatriated. I doubt if anybody has read this before. So now for the first time I can reveal what was going on at the Mid Wales Mental Hospital when most of it was taken over by the Army between 1941–1947.

This book is not a simple history of the Mid Wales Mental Hospital. It is intended to show how we treated mentally ill people over the twentieth century, with the focus on the Mid Wales. It is a story well worth telling. The Mid Wales was a major institution on the Welsh landscape and it exemplified orthodox treatment over 100 years, from asylum to community care. This is an important subject today. I hesitate to add, though I will add, that if we don't know our history we are condemned to repeat it.

A postcard of Talgarth Asylum in 1909, taken from the east side, with the main north entrance superimposed in the bottom right corner

Chapter One
Life in the Asylum

The new asylum

Wednesday 27 February 1903 was a glorious day, spring-like in the manner beloved of the poet, and from early hours large numbers of people began to pour into Talgarth and wend their way up the hill to the asylum.

It was the opening day of the Brecknock and Radnor Joint Asylum, and the reporter of the *Brecon County Times* shared in the excitement. The asylum was 'up top', above but invisible from Talgarth, and this soon became its nickname in the town. It has an obvious double meaning – in the same way that asylums on the outskirts of towns were placed out of sight: 'round the bend'. Mental illness attracts these metaphors that reveal our fascination and fear of what may happen to any of us.

The crowds were intent on inspecting every nook and corner of an institution they probably only heard about from highly sensational novels, whose description of such buildings was more calculated to curdle the blood than give an idea of their true character. Inquiries as to the locale of the padded cells were so incessant as to inspire anyone with the idea that as a people we are getting increasingly morbid, yet all other portions of the well-appointed building received the attention they deserved.

The site was ideal. Located 'under the scowling brow of Mynydd Troed', in the Black Mountains, it was sheltered from the north and east winds. The new road to Talgarth connected it to the railway station and the world beyond. The ground had belonged to Chancefield Farm, purchased for

Workmen wearing their Sunday best at the opening of the asylum

£7,250, and the adjoining farm of Wern Fawr encompassed a total of 300 acres. It was, the reporter enthused, 'one of the best sites in the county, ensuring utmost privacy while allowing the inmates, many of whom are the agricultural classes, boundless opportunities for profitable recreation in the way of kitchen gardening'.

The asylum had taken 300 men three years to build. The buildings themselves covered seven acres and were constructed from local stone quarried above the site and carried down on a tramway; the full trucks down the hill were propelled by gravity and restrained by brakes and their weight was sufficient to pull the empty trucks up the other side. The asylum was constructed using 3 million bricks made on site, the exterior being faced with stone. The roofs were slate. Many small-paned windows attracted the light and provided views of green hills; but none of them opened more than 4 inches. Plentiful water came from the Enig Brook, filtered through a settling bed, stored in a reservoir and carried to any part of the building by gravity. Extra soft rainwater for the vast laundries came off the roofs and was channelled into a large tank. The asylum generated its own electricity; the Medical Superintendent could make a complete tour of the building after dark by lighting himself through and switching off lights without retracing his steps. An engine house stoked two large boilers to develop steam, which heated the entire institution and gave hot water for laundry.

The kitchens showed the asylum belonged to the twentieth century because, said the reporter, 'Every modern facility for cooking is noticeable'. There was a tea infuser capable of boiling water for 100 gallons of tea in 15 minutes. There was a beef-tea kettle holding 30 gallons, and a potato steamer that could cook 3 cwt of potatoes in 15 minutes! The laundries, for there were three of them – 'foul' (where nothing was washed by hand), 'officers' and 'general' – boasted equally impressive statistics: 39 moveable drying horses, three washing machines, three wringers, a large ironing machine and two mangles driven by electricity, and a stove capable of heating 40 irons at the same time. The asylum was fireproof, with hydrants placed on every floor.

The *Brecon County Times* gave its verdict:

> It has been said that we house our paupers better than our labourers, and our criminals better than either. The impression one gains as one walks over the asylum is that our imbeciles have more comforts than all put together.

The Brecknock and Radnor Joint Asylum was designed by the prolific architectural practice of Giles, Gough and Trollope of London; the builder was Watkin Williams of Pontypridd. The familiar asylum design resembled what became known as the butterfly shape. The long body began with an imposing entrance hall notable for its polished pitch-pine floor covered with rugs, continued with the administration offices, then kitchen and dining or recreation hall that could accommodate 500, and beyond a courtyard lay the staff quarters. These were connected by corridors, totalling one third of a mile in length with intercommunication by

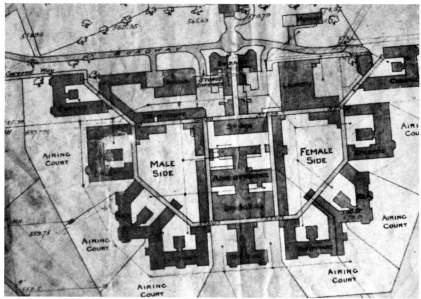

First ground plan of the asylum, in the shape of a butterfly

telephone. The corridors also connected with the two wings of the
butterfly, one the male side and the other female. Each wing had three
'ward pavilions' on two floors with their own 'airing court,' a secure garden
where patients could 'take the air'.

There were six male wards on the West side, and six female on the
East, both halves identical but designed for different types of patient:
Recent and Acute, Chronic, Epileptic, Infirm (described by our reporter
as 'cases of harmless idiocy and senile decay' – these were on the ground
floor), and the otherwise sick. As time went on, the incurability and
institutionalisation of many patients meant that at least 60 per cent of the
beds at Talgarth were taken up by the elderly infirm, many of them
bedridden. The two halves, male and female, were strictly segregated for
staff and patients. Even the mortuary had a male and female side. It could,
said our reporter, have the inscription above the doorway: 'Divided even
in Death'. Only at post-mortem did the sexes share the same slab.

Matron Chipchase and her attendants in a ward day room

The asylum was small as asylums went, designed for 350 patients with the capacity to expand to 500. That meant that the 12 wards at their fullest each housed between 20 and 40 patients – and 'housed' is the right word, as the ward became the home. Patients slept in dormitories called 'Nightingale wards', with side rooms for those who required more security; they ate and socialised in the day rooms attached. Each ward had toilet and washing facilities and sluices. There were four padded cells, two for men and two for women. The Dining Hall, with its fine arched roof supported by pilasters, was also used for entertainments, and later as a cinema.

Across a sweeping drive were a substantial chapel and a mortuary; slightly removed from the principal buildings there was an isolation ward for infectious diseases like TB and typhoid. Attached to the main building, a series of purpose-built workshops provided a bakery, a butchery, a tailor's shop, a shoemaker, a printer; there was even a photographic dark room. From the outset there was an eight-acre market garden, farm buildings, and Chancefield House itself, where the Medical Superintendent lived with his

Misses Dunant as Spanish Dancer
& One of "Forty Thieves.

The Misses Dunant perform at the Asylum

family. Unique in the Talgarth area, probably, was the asylum's own steam-powered lorry, used to transport coal up the hill from the station.

The whole edifice, substantial and in many ways self-sufficient, was built at a cost of only £126,000, since the stone, sand, clay and water came free. Bearing in mind the isolation and poverty of this small Welsh community of Talgarth, the asylum was a colossal achievement, an expression of Edwardian optimism and Welsh determination. It put Talgarth on the map and became its sole employer of any size. Its like will never be seen again. It is hoped that is how the hospital is remembered in the town, rather than as the disgraceful ruin it became within a few years of its closure.

Five thousand people attended the opening ceremony. In the evening Mr Watkin Williams, the builder, entertained all his workmen to dinner and a concert. As our reporter noted, it had been a glorious day. Then the patients began to arrive. One of the very first, a private patient, drove up in a pony and trap from Abergavenny. He was still a patient at Talgarth in the 1950s, half a century later.

Laws for lunatics

The asylum soon filled. The national census of 1911 recorded 361 patients, of whom 170 were male and 191 female, an imbalance in favour of women that was to remain throughout the Mid Wales Hospital's history. There were also some children, one as young as six. Nearly all, perhaps 90 per cent, were paupers, meaning that they were paid for by the Poor Law rates. Most of the men were Labourers by occupation; most of the women, when they had occupations at all, were Domestic Servants. There was a scattering of private patients such as a bank manager, a clergyman, a grocer, a sculptor, a surgeon and the captain of a tugboat. Asylums everywhere were predominantly for the poor because such was the stigma attached to such institutions that those with money either arranged for private care at home or for entry into the few private asylums. This must have been particularly true in the poor counties of mid Wales.

That the Brecknock and Radnor Joint Asylum was built at all was due to the 1845 Lunatic Asylums Act, revised in 1890. This created a national system of care for pauper lunatics based on a uniform model. Henceforth, sufficient accommodation was to be provided by every county or city – and over the next half century or so over 60 asylums were built, the Brecknock and Radnor being one of the last. In fact, it was a breakaway from the Lunatic Asylum at Abergavenny, later known as Pen-y-Fal Hospital, that served the additional counties of Hereford and Monmouthshire. By the 1870s this was overflowing, having over 700 patients so that Brecknockshire and Radnorshire planned a second asylum shared between them, and Montgomeryshire joined in 1921.

Quite why the amount of mental illness in the Western world increased so rapidly in the second half of the nineteenth century is not clear, though the new availability of asylum space had a lot to do with it. In England the rate of confinement of the mentally ill more than doubled, from 1.6 to 3.7 per thousand of the adult population. Before the Asylums Act of 1845 only about 5,000 'lunatics' were cared for in publicly-funded asylums while a further 12,000 languished in prison or workhouse and many others remained untreated at home, like the Mad Woman of *Kilvert's Diary*. At the end of the nineteenth century about 100,000 'lunatics' were patients in the new asylums.

The Lunacy Act gave power to the Commissioners in Lunacy, who produced rules that imposed uniformity on the treatment of 'the mad or lunatic', as the mentally ill were called: how public asylums should be built, how patients should be cared for, how their cases should be reported. At a local level, a Visiting Committee of worthies was empowered to operate the Act and the Minutes of their visits to the Brecknock and Radnor Asylum have provided me with much of this information.

This is how the Act worked: an individual suspected of being mentally ill and without means of 'relief' (financial support) to pay for confinement in an asylum was reported to the relieving officer of the neighbourhood Poor Law Union (the Union was simply a geographical term covering the parishes involved). This report might come from a family, or from the police who may have picked up a vagrant or suspected criminal and summoned him or her to the magistrates' court. The relieving officer worked with the medical officer attached to the local workhouse or 'spike', the dreaded institution that provided accommodation and work for the otherwise destitute – most towns had a workhouse, including Brecon, Hay, Crickhowell and Abergavenny. If the two found evidence of insanity then they would call for the opinion of another doctor, and if he concurred, then the 'lunatic', for that would now be his or her status, could be committed to an asylum by a local Justice of the Peace.

Once in the asylum there was no fixed term for confinement. Unless you were a voluntary private patient discharge depended upon the asylum staff, though appeal could be made to the Visiting Committee:

> September 1908
> Mrs B—— accompanied by her Brother and Brother-in-Law made a personal application [to the Brecknock and Radnor Joint Asylum] for the discharge of patient H——. The Committee after interviewing the patient RESOLVED that H—— was a fit person for detention in the Asylum. The Chairman informed Mrs B—— of this resolution and advised her not to apply again as the patient would be discharged at once if in a fit state. But if she was still desirous of taking the matter further she could lay the case before the Commissioners in Lunacy.

What was the rate of discharge? Data for asylums as a whole show that very few long-stay patients were ever discharged. The percentage for new admissions was a lot higher, as one would expect. One in three patients who entered the Brecknock and Radnor Asylum would be released within a year, although many of these might find themselves returning. Before release they would be given parole, meaning that they were freer than other patients to walk in the grounds and even into Talgarth. On release they were given a suit of clothes and a month's allowance, if necessary. However, the fact that many patients were in the asylum until death – and this figure would rise incrementally – would determine the character of the hospital throughout its history.

The Lunacy Act of 1845 was well-intentioned. The new asylums should be 'fixed upon an airy and healthy situation' (the Brecknock and Radnor certainly qualified here) and provide modern facilities. This was the early period of the 'cult of curability', when progressive minds considered that placing the mentally ill in therapeutic isolation and showing them kindness, and restraint when needed, would speed recovery. For this treatment the rate-aided patients received three times as much as the pauper in the workhouse; there was a moral behind this. The self-help Victorian ethos blamed the poor as workshy, but accepted the mad as not to blame; they were 'deserving poor'.

The General Ledgers of the Brecknock and Radnor record in detail the poor law contributions from the rate payers of Brecon, Crickhowell, Hay, Builth, Merthyr Tydfil and other Union towns. This money covered the costs of maintenance including funerals, 'fetchings and removals', furniture and bedding, rent of telephones, books and periodicals and winding clocks, wines and spirits, the cost of produce from the farm and the cost of maintaining the gardens. These costs tripled between 1906 and 1921 to 36 shillings per patient per week.

Throughout the history of the Mid Wales, incidentally, the food was reported to be excellent. In 1906 payment was made to Wern Fawr farm for 170 lbs of lamb, 10,246 lbs of mutton, 8,491 lbs of pork and 1,475 lbs of beef, 10,325 gallons of milk and 485 cwt of potatoes. Physically life was healthy whatever the mental condition. Wern Fawr farm was sold in 1955 but the standard of food remained high, a tribute in part to the local suppliers in Talgarth.

However, the asylum system as conceived in 1845 was much abused. By the time the Brecknock and Radnor was opened in 1903, asylums had come to be considered, with prisons and workhouses, as a triumvirate of Poor Law institutions, with human traffic flowing between them. Prisons contained convicts who behaved like lunatics; workhouses looked after the agèd who were mentally infirm. It was all too easy to incarcerate these outcasts from society in the new asylum, which had the additional advantage for the police of collecting up these outcasts from remote country areas so that they were, at least, in one place. Thus as the asylums entered the twentieth century they came to be regarded by critics as the dustbins of society: 'loony bins', in short.

The Lunacy Act was updated in 1890 and lasted until 1959. Just as significant for asylums was the Mental Deficiency Act of 1913, introduced following a report by the Royal Commission on the Care and Control of the Feeble-Minded. It was discussed at length by the Visiting Committee of the Brecknock and Radnor Asylum and duly minuted. At this time the medical diagnosis of 'congenital insanity', as opposed to mental illness, covered several inherited and incurable conditions like 'idiocy', 'imbecility' and 'feeble-mindedness'. The Act proposed that these 'mental defectives' should be separated from the mentally ill, taken out of asylums and workhouses and placed in special 'colonies'.

This was well-meaning, but there were those who feared that this might result in the application of the fashionable thinking of eugenics, the belief that the genetic stock of society would be improved by preventing the congenitally insane from breeding. This led in Nazi Germany to the sterilisation and gassing of over 70,000 mental defectives, beginning in 1939. This did not happen here, and hospitals for the congenitally insane or mentally defective were established, though nothing like enough. In mid Wales there were two that later came under the management of the Mid Wales Hospital, Llys Maldwyn at Caersws and Brynhyfryd at Forden. The Commission concluded that 0.46 per cent of the British population came into this category, amounting at that time to 150,000 people.

It is a fact that throughout the history of the Mid Wales Asylum and then Mental Hospital many patients were stuck there who were

Head Attendant Albert Fawke

mentally defective but not strictly speaking mentally ill. What to do with them was a constant theme in Visiting Committee Minutes. Former nurses acknowledge them with a weary acceptance. Dr Diggle, who was Medical Superintendent at the Mid Wales in the 1950s and 60s, lightened the gloom by remarking that the best thing that happened in the rural areas of mid Wales was the arrival of the motorbike, because it opened up remote communities that were inbred. There was some truth in this. In inner Wales near Welshpool, in the north of the area covered by the asylum, lies 'Mad Valley', so described on a map in a book in the Mid Wales library. The grandchildren of Head Attendant Albert Fawke, themselves later nurses at Talgarth, remember him pointing out the locations plotted on the map where lived families with mentally deficient members who had ended up in one institution or another. The saying went:

Rhayader man born and bred,
Strong in the arm and weak in the head.

It was the new definition of 'moral imbecile' in the 1913 Act that was pernicious: 'Displaying mental weakness coupled with strong vicious or criminal propensities, and on whom punishment has little or no effect'. This was dangerously open to abuse, so that it came to be regarded all too often as an instrument of social control. For example, the phrase 'moral imbecile' led to the strong suspicion that young women were incarcerated because they had illegitimate babies. Every former female nurse at the Mid Wales I spoke to knew of such patients who had been committed 'up top' many years before, whether under the Mental Deficiency Act or not. Delcie Davies, who became the Manager of the Mid Wales in the 1980s but who began as a secretary in 1948, assured me that she had knowledge of such cases from the personal files. Of course, it's hard to prove. Did the young mother perhaps suffer from post-natal depression because her baby had been taken away? Or were her parents ashamed of the stigma attached to illegitimacy in those days and wanted her out of the way? Perhaps both,

as in this case recorded by Gladys Davies, who was a nurse at Talgarth
between 1949–1968:

> A farmer's daughter had been brought in as a patient in her
> early twenties. Her parents were elderly and it was their
> custom to go to Brecon market and leave their daughter at
> home on the farm. Working on the farm was a Polish ex-
> prisoner-of-war and eventually it was found that the
> daughter was pregnant by him. The mother took a very hard
> line giving her daughter many hidings and insisting that
> when the baby was born it was put out for adoption. This
> happened. The daughter became quite violent and was
> committed to the Mid Wales where she was put on F3, a
> somewhat rough ward with epileptics. She would attack
> other patients, particularly the elderly who could not defend
> themselves. Eventually she settled down and was moved to a
> better ward and allowed out on parole.
>
> She had a very warm and lovable nature and was
> affectionate – if she had been allowed to keep her baby she
> would, no doubt, have been an excellent mother. She was artistic
> and would draw scenes of tractors and farm animals. One day
> she said to me, very profoundly, 'Life is passing me by'.

The reality of life in Mid Wales in the old days was that if the patient's
family did not visit or want a release, and as personal records were denied
to the nurses until the 1970s, it was all too easy for a patient to fester over
the years and become institutionalised. This was true particularly if you
were a voluntary patient or committed before 1959, when the Mental
Health Act gave the right for periodic review of patients who had been
committed. Here is a truly sad case: Dr Michael Hession, who became a
Senior Consultant at the Mid Wales in the 1970s, told me of a very elderly
male patient who, as a young teenager before the Great War, had been

caught 'flashing' in Talgarth market place. He had been incarcerated ever since, his whole life wasted in a mental hospital; and by the time Dr Hession discovered him he was too old and frail to live anywhere else. Here is another case: a nurse in the late 1970s remembers looking up a patient's file and reading that the cause of consigning him to the Mid Wales asylum many, many years before was 'Found wandering on ? Moor and making no sense'. There must have been many vagrants who ended up in the Mid Wales this way.

The good intentions of the 1845 and 1890 Lunacy Acts and the 1913 Mental Deficiency Act, therefore, were undermined by their application. There were many patients in the asylums who should not have been there: the criminal but sane, the mentally defective and, no doubt, many 'moral imbeciles' too. There was one further category. On 25 June 1910 the Visiting Committee at the Brecknock and Radnor sent a letter to the Guardians of the Poor Law Union in the Counties of Brecon and Radnorshire 'pointing out that very aged patients are sent to the Asylum from the Workhouses in these Counties who on reception here are found to show no mental derangement other than those which accompany great age and which should not obviate such cases being dealt with in a Workhouse'. One such case that tugs the heart strings was a former clergyman, a private patient, suffering from senile decay aged 82. The Patients' Book says: 'He is quiet, sensibly managed and could well benefit from a single room outside the Asylum'. He was paying 22 shillings a month.

The patients

In his book *Life in the Victorian Asylum*, Mark Stevens collected together the observations of doctors that led them to the diagnosis of insanity:

- Incessant chatter and the use of inappropriate or over-familiar language, laughing or singing without obvious cause or motive.

- A loss of strength or will, resulting in a failure to be active in chores or employment or to interact with those around you.
- A belief that fraudulent enemies unknown are depriving you of something that is rightfully yours, or trying to poison or otherwise attack you. Typically, a patient in this condition may have made threats to harm someone they know or destroy their property, believing them to be part of the conspiracy against them.
- Being found wandering without seeming to have an aim or direction, and usually in a state of inadequate dress.
- A fear or dread of something being about to befall you, no matter how unlikely, such as your bed catching fire or your breathing suddenly to cease.
- Holding some unusual desires or notions, such as the need to act as a messenger or a belief that you are a new prophet.
- Unusual facial expressions, such as constant grimacing, twitching or violent movements or the acting out of imaginary fancies.
- Being a parent, especially a mother, who ceases to show interest in the care of her children. In extreme case, threatening or attempting to harm her child.

At a time before the term schizophrenia had been invented, most of the insane were labelled as suffering from some sort of mania. This 'mania' often showed what we now call bipolar symptoms, the patient moving from extreme excitability to extreme depression. I have chosen four examples from the earliest Discharges and Deaths files of the Brecknock and Radnor Joint Asylum which contain detailed medical notes and photographs. All the cases are over 100 years old and no patient is identified by name.

Case One

Miss A.B, a domestic servant. Diagnosis: Hysterical Mania. When I [the medical officer] *visited her she was very excited and restless, going from room to room and looking out through the window, remarking that her young man was passing by. Then she broke out with laughter. She is very violent. Hit her father with a poker and cut the arm of her mother with a knife. Breaks things in the house.*

Later, after admission: *She is restless, amorous and erotic, very hysterical. States people are against her and do not want her to marry her young man; a good deal of hysteria.*

She died after one year in the asylum, aged 22. The verdict was hereditary insanity, for several of her family had been patients in Abergavenny asylum.

Case 2

Miss C.D. Diagnosis: Religious mania. Very excited and loquacious. Exhibits signs of religious mania, talking about the crucifixion of her family. She has visions of the Holy Spirit and believes she is one of the blessed, and all other people are wicked. She calls herself Miss La Neve. She shouts constantly sentences with scriptural ideas and phrases like 'bottomless pit' and 'Satan'. Imagines she is an evangelical preacher.

She was discharged after one year as 'recovered'.

Note: These files contain several cases of religious mania. It is very tempting to connect these with the town of Talgarth, which had been a centre for Methodist Revival since the days of the charismatic preacher Hywel Harris. Methodists invested mental turmoil with profound spiritual significance. Anxiety, despair, guilt and fear were bound up with the perils of damnation and the promise of salvation, the struggle between the Divine and the temptations of Evil. Illnesses of the mind were associated with divine retribution and demoniacal possession. It is easy to see the effect of this on an impressionable young woman.

Case 3

Miss E.F., a domestic servant. Diagnosis: Acutely Maniacal. She shouts, laughs, has delusions of identity, strips herself of all clothing. She remains in a padded cell as she struggles violently with nurses.

She was discharged in 1911 after one year as 'recovered'.

Case 4

Mr G.H. Diagnosis: sub-acute mania with major illusions. He says he is in the Dragoon Guards, that he was a hairdresser, manicurist, train conductor and had served a major appointment on the Mauritania [a passenger liner]. *He is insolent and abusive.*

He was transferred to another asylum.

Note: Perhaps another diagnosis of Case 4 would be 'monomania'. The patient was convinced he had a variety of occupations but otherwise he was not insane. His intellect and reasoning seemed normal until he turned to his delusions of employment.

The twin of mania was melancholia, an extreme of depression leading to suicidal tendencies and an appearance of sadness without a spark of life. Melancholics are self-aware and able to describe their symptoms graphically. I have chosen two private voluntary patients.

Case 5

Mrs I.J., married, a housewife. Diagnosis: A melancholic. She is listless, dejected, depressed; actively suicidal with imperfect knowledge of her surroundings.

She was removed from the asylum by her husband.

Case 6

Mr K.L., a grocer. Diagnosis: Acutely depressed. He imagines he is ruined and that God and man have turned against him. He thinks he is 'done for'. He has a wound in his throat and is in great misery.

He recovered and discharged himself after one year.

And here is a patient who today would clearly be diagnosed as schizophrenic:

Case 7

Mrs M.N. Diagnosis: She suffers from auditory hallucinations and delusional insanity. She hears voices speaking to her through imaginary telephones. She runs round the house quite naked at night. She has many delusions of persecution. She states that people are trying to burn down her house.

She was discharged at the request of her husband as 'recovered'.

One-fifth of the patients in asylums suffered from General Paralysis of the Insane, known as GPI. In 1910 its cause was unknown. Only a few years later, after spectacular experiments in Austria that involved injecting the patient with malaria causing fever that destroyed syphilitic germs in the brain, it was proved that the cause was biological, and a cure was occasionally possible. GPI was a symptom of tertiary syphilis. This terrible disease led to paralysis of speech and movement, the inability to swallow and control the bowels. It destroyed the mind too. GPI was even more terrible because men passed it on to women (and vice versa) through sex. There were cases of GPI in the Brecknock and Radnor throughout its history. Here is one example:

Case 8

Mr P.Q., a boiler-maker. Diagnosis: GPI. Has delusions he is captain of a ship; wild expressions; lost in time and space.

He died within a year of entering the asylum.

Another common type of insanity in the asylum was dementia (or 'loss of mind'), with which we are all too familiar today. Dementia is progressive and the onset is usually late in life, unlike imbecility which is present from birth. It is often accompanied by 'filthy habits' that require a lot of nursing. Here is one case, though the young age – hard to believe – is not typical:

Case 9

Mr R.S., a labourer aged 30. Diagnosis: Dementia Paralytica. He is syphilitic and alcoholic with filthy habits. He attacks other patients. Looks about 60. Suffers from loss of mind.

He died within the year of entry into the asylum.

There were enough epileptics in the asylum to fill one male and one female ward, and these were equipped with softer furnishings and lower chairs and beds. Today, epilepsy is treated by medication or surgery, and is certainly not regarded as a form of insanity. One hundred years ago the boundary was not at all clear, as in this example:

Case 10

Mr T.W. Diagnosis: Epileptic Insanity. After a fit gets excited and then becomes dull and confused for days. A raving lunatic. Takes three men to hold him when in this state.

He died after a few years in the asylum.

Many cases were diagnosed as 'congenital insanity', but this is the only case between 1909–1916 of a child:

Case 11

Master X.Y. Aged 6. Diagnosis: Congenital insanity. He is evidently of unsound mind; screams without cause. Pushes a stick into babies' mouths with great force and quite unsafe to leave with other children. Vicious.

He died a year after entry.

The Eighteenth Annual Report of the Committee of Visitors at the Joint Lunatic Asylum at Talgarth in March 1921 stated that 61 patients had been admitted the previous year. Of these, 29 suffered from congenital mental deficiency, 19 from melancholia, 13 from mania, five from dementia, four from delusional insanity, three from general paralysis of the insane and one from insanity with epilepsy.

The attendants

In the days of the asylum the staff were called 'attendants' and not nurses. What's in a name? In this case it is an important distinction: the attendant's job was to supervise patients and not to nurse them in a medical sense. Little treatment was offered except physical exercise and the sedation of bromide pills, while supervision could mean the difference between life and death or injury.

The 1911 census records that 26 asylum attendants lived 'up top', of whom 17 were female. Presumably there were other attendants who were married and lived outside so they were not included in this census. All asylums found it easier to recruit female staff, partly because many had worked before as domestic servants and partly because the pay for that work was bad. In 1915 the starting salary for a male attendant was £28 per year, though, presumably, if he lived in the asylum his accommodation and food was at least subsidised.

The asylum staff system was hierarchical from the Medical Superintendent downwards. The very first Medical Superintendent was Dr W. Ernest Jones ('a gentleman with considerable experience in lunacy', said the *Brecon County Times*), but he left within a year to become Inspector General of the Insane for the Colony of Victoria in Australia. He has a curious claim to fame which I shall reveal shortly. He was succeeded by Dr Robert Pugh, at a salary of £400 per year. Below him was another medical practitioner, Assistant Medical Officer Dr Perdran. There was a head attendant on the male side and a matron on the female side; under them, charge attendants on the male side and sisters on the female, meaning that they were each responsible for a ward – and so on. As the photo of Matron Chipchase and her staff shows, female attendants wore starched white caps, and ankle-length white aprons tied at the waist, over blue dresses. Male attendants wore dark blue caps with dark blue suits. The male charge attendants and the head attendant carried gold braid on their caps and jackets, while the female attendants displayed their

Matron Chipchase with her attendants

rank with a coloured ribbon round their caps. I was told that in the old days, nurses' caps required special ironing with separate styles for matron, sisters and other nurses; also that the asylum tailor used to sew all the uniforms for the staff, made-to-measure after just one fitting.

Life in the asylum was governed by rules. The *Rules for the Management of the Brecon and Radnorshire Asylum* of 1904 were signed by Lord Glanusk, the Chairman of the Committee of Visitors, and there was no doubt that his intentions were well meaning, his ambition noble: 'Everything has been done that human ingenuity could devise for the happiness and safety of the inmates'. The records in the County Archive show how rigorously these rules were enforced. Whatever Lord Glanusk's sentiments, life in the asylum was dangerous and volatile, and it was the attendants who carried the heavy burden of responsibility on the wards.

Rule 1
The Male and Female patients shall be kept in separate wards and no male attendant shall be allowed to enter the female side without authority. Any attendant transgressing this rule shall be immediately dismissed. No male person except the Medical Officers shall have a key to female wards.

Rule 3
No wards occupied by patients shall be left at any time without an attendant.

Rule 4
As a principle of treatment, endeavours shall be continuously made to occupy the patients, to induce them to take exercise in the open air, and to promote cheerfulness and happiness among them.

Rule 9
No patient on any account whatever shall be struck or threatened and no patient shall be kept in seclusion except by order of the Superintendent, unless in cases of extreme violence. On no account must knees be placed on the body or limbs twisted.

Note: Visiting Committee Hearing in 1937: Patient G.H. had complained that Probationer Male Nurse G.M. had struck him several blows and during the same incident Staff Nurse W.C. had intervened and struck him roughly. Male Nurse G.M. admitted striking the patient one blow under great provocation. He was dismissed forthwith, but Staff Nurse W.C. was exonerated.

Rule 10

Mechanical restraint shall not be used except upon the direction in writing of the Medical Superintendent. Every direction shall be entered in the Order Book, with a counterfoil, giving exact times for which restraint is directed.

Note: The Register of Mechanical Restraint 1903–1954: In the 1920s and 30s the straitjacket and/or padded cell were resorted to between four and ten times per year. Most of the patients so restrained were female. The reasons given were 'noisy and violent behaviour' and 'attempts to mutilate herself'. The duration for mechanical restraint averaged 4–5 hours with a maximum of 10 hours.

Rule 12

Any accident, however slight, attempts to escape or commit suicide and struggles between patients and attendants should be reported to Head Attendants.

Note: The Casualty Report Book for Ward M[ale] 4 for 1911: This must have been a chronic ward, or one for epileptics because it reports 76 casualties that year: casualties self-inflicted or inflicted on others. They included these distressing examples: 'falling down in a fit'; 'striking another patient and scratching his face'; 'throwing himself on the floor, lying on his back and kicking anyone who comes near him'; 'springing up and grabbing another patient violently by the throat'; 'attacked other patients this morning, struck two severe blows causing black eye and bleeding nose'; 'fell out of bed in a fit and damaged his eye, kicking and biting'.

An attendant recorded:

Patient P.H. became very violent this afternoon by striking and kicking at me whilst in the airing court. Attendants T., J., B. and C. came to my assistance and with great difficulty

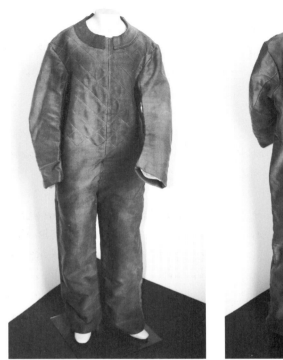

A moleskin suit from the Mid Wales Mental Hospital

he was placed in a padded room. He has a swelling on the right side of his face and marks on the backs of his hands from biting himself.

Violent patients with a self-destructive mania were dressed in a moleskin suit that buttoned down the back so it could not be ripped off.

Rule 13
All attendants shall treat their patients kindly and shall not speak harshly to them. They shall be responsible for the safety, cleanliness and general condition of patients or be liable for instant dismissal.

Rule 15

Relatives may be allowed to visit any day of the week except Sunday between 10 and 12 and 2 and 4, no visit beyond one hour. Patients shall be at liberty to hold private conversations but no male shall remain in a room with a female except in the presence of an attendant.

Rule 16

No stranger shall be admitted into any part of the asylum occupied by a patient except by authority of the law.

The following year, 1905, the Asylum issued *General Rules for Attendants and Nurses* based on the Lunacy Act of 1890. There were 61 rules that show a zeal for laying down the law that must have seemed intimidating to a local lad working 'up top' for the first time; an example of the Victorian mind believing that by rationalising behaviour it was bound to improve. Behind the words it is easy to imagine what day-to-day life must have been like:

Rule 3

Attendants are responsible for keys and are prohibited from handing them to a patient in any circumstances. They are strictly enjoined, having opened the door, to lock it again afterwards: closed quietly and not slammed.

Ken Morgan became a nurse in 1952 and recollects clearly when he was given his key with its own number. This remained in his possession until he left: it was his symbol of office. He remembers his key opened all male wards, while other former nurses think it only opened their ward. The charge nurse had a pass key, a light key, since lights were not operated by a switch – Rule 46: *Attendants must not allow patients to touch electric light controls* – and a cupboard key. There were at least two locked cupboards; what Ken Morgan refers to as the 'Black Box' meaning the cupboard where all the cutlery was stored, counted out and then counted back after meals, and the medicine cupboard. Only the most senior staff had keys that opened both male and female wards. (If there was any one symbolic moment at the Mid Wales when modern treatment of the mentally ill replaced the old system, then it was in the late 1970s when most wards were opened up.)

Rule 6

The attendants must see that the patient is washed, combed and properly dressed in the morning before passing to the day room. All feeble and helpless patients require the active assistance of the attendant.

Rule 7

The patients are to have a regular change of stockings and underclothes weekly. Any soiled clothing to be changed without delay.

The patients wore their own clothes, not a uniform, and when these became unwearable they were replenished from a stock kept on each ward.

Rule 10

All religious scruples are to be respected. In Chapel, those who are restless and troublesome must be seated near an attendant. At the commencement of meals, as well as the close, grace must be said, all standing in a becoming manner.

The asylum had its own Chaplain, in the early years the Rev. T.L. Davies, who served also as informal teacher and librarian. It was he who brought the newspapers up from Talgarth and provided a store of books.

Rule 17

The patients must be taught to occupy their seats in the proper manner. They are not permitted to sit or lie on the floor, crouch in corners or loiter in the sanitary annexes.

Rule 18

All unemployed patients must go into the Airing Courts at the appointed hour. Attention must be paid to melancholic, indolent and listless cases, so that they do not fall into the habit of remaining indoors.

Rule 19

In their walks around the grounds, patients are not allowed to tread on the flower beds. Those with morbid habits must be prevented from eating leaves or lying down in the flower beds.

Rule 33

All patients entered on the ward list as having 'suicidal propensities' require to be under constant supervision day and night. At night the whole of their clothing must be removed from sleeping apartments and nothing must be concealed about their bedding. All persons suffering from melancholia are to be regarded as of suicidal tendency.

A Suicidal Caution Card was pinned above the bed of the patient concerned and staff on that ward were required to sign that they had read it. One example, dated May 29 1932, is in Brecon Museum. Ken Morgan remembers being shown the 'Red Card' list of potential suicides on his ward by the Charge Nurse every morning.

Nevertheless, throughout the history of the Mid Wales very few patients did commit suicide. In the early days these suicides were reported by the *Brecon County Times*. In one horrible case a female patient working

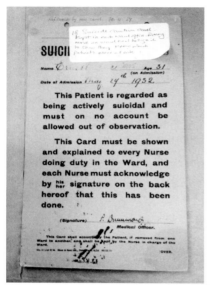

The Suicide Caution Card front and back

in the laundry threw herself into a vat of boiling water and was scalded to death. In another a male patient on probation threw himself in front of a train at Talgarth Station.

Patients escaped too:

TALGARTH LUNATIC CAPTURED.

M.J. who escaped from the Talgarth asylum on the 4th inst. was captured on Saturday not far from Brecon. She had subsisted on what she could pick up from the ground like raw potatoes and turnips. She was in an emaciated condition.

Rule 59

No attendant may get married without the sanction of the Medical Superintendent.

28 March 1908

Gentlemen of the Visiting Committee,

I respectfully beg permission to be allowed to get married. Hoping this application will receive your favourable consideration,

I beg to remain, Gentlemen, Your Obedient Servant, F. M.

His application was granted, with the assurance that he could live outside the grounds; but he was not entitled to any increase in purchasing from the asylum stores.

Rule 61

Attendants render themselves liable to instant dismissal for any act of misconduct such as carelessness or neglect of duties... ill-treatment of any patient... immoral conduct and intoxication within and without the Asylum.

The Mid Wales Hospital in the 1920s

In a 'total institution', where both staff and patients were cut off from the outside world for a considerable time, and lived in close proximity, there must have been a strong temptation for sexual activity, despite or perhaps because of the formal separation of the sexes. And eroticism was a symptom of mental illness in some patients. Cases of sexual harassment appear to have been rare, but one concerned the Assistant Medical Officer himself. In 1912 a ward sister accused Dr Joseph Perdran in a letter to the Visiting Committee:

> On Friday last, whilst in the recreation hall, I refused Dr Perdran the Staff Dance. After putting my patients to bed I went into Female No 4 Store Room and he came in and insulted me by calling me names detrimental to my character. He said I was a mad brain insane lunatic and I was cracked because I refused to dance with him.

It turned out that the A.M.O. had been asked to resign from a previous appointment and had not admitted that in his application to Talgarth. He was dismissed and left the next day.

A truly upsetting case was reported fully in the *Brecon County Times* in May 1910. It concerned a 'nurse-attendant' at Talgarth, and it is worth reporting because the offence shows the sort of 'demented' behaviour that could have been associated with an asylum patient. At Talgarth Police Court she was accused of having sent the body of her recently-born female child in the post to her lover in Northamptonshire. In the parcel was her letter:

> Oh, Arthur, I don't know how to tell you but the other night I gave birth to a child. Oh Arthur, I was in trouble and didn't know it. Not a soul knows of it. I bore it all alone. Oh Arthur, whatever should I have done had it been alive? You will be able to bury it, won't you?
>
> When shall I come to see you Arthur, dear? You are my husband now.

She was sent to the Assizes for trial. The paper reported that the couple had married at Hay Registry Office just before the court appearance, which shines a bright light on this dark tale.

The treatment

The word 'asylum' means a refuge from the evils of society, and this is what the asylums were. The Commissioners in Lunacy believed that to remove a lunatic from the environment that had made him mad was the first stage of treatment. The second stage was to provide a caring, calm and secure regime. The third was to guarantee the therapeutic qualities of fresh air. This is why the location and design of the asylum at Talgarth had been chosen. Hence the 'Rules for the Management' specified:

Rule 4

As a principle of treatment, endeavours shall be continually made to occupy the patients, to induce them to take exercise in the open air, and to promote cheerfulness and happiness among them.

Rule 5

During the day the patients shall be employed as much as practicable in suitable occupations out of doors.

Rule 7

Such patients as the Superintendent shall direct shall be allowed to take walks or make excursions beyond the walls of the Asylum. The airing courts shall be open to patients every day, whenever the weather is favourable.

The daily routine was structured around meals on the wards: breakfast at 7 (8 in winter) consisting of 8 oz. of sliced brown wheat bread, baked on the premises, butter and jam, washed down with cups of tea; dinner at 12.30, a substantial meal of meat, veg and pudding, much of it provided at Talgarth by the farm and garden; tea at 5 or 6 that was a replication of breakfast.

The daily work involved all those who could be productive, perhaps half the patients. There would be cleaning, scrubbing and polishing parties on the wards for both sexes. Within living memory, the floor polisher was known as a 'bumper', that is a long-handled wide brush to which wax would be applied. The female patients who were active and able went to the kitchen, laundries or sewing room, and the men to the farm or gardens. Those with the skills of the trade would assist the baker, tailor, shoemaker and butcher (though there was no abattoir). This was useful occupational therapy that also made Talgarth as self-sufficient as possible. Chairbound, bedbound, untrustworthy or incapable patients remained on the wards, where the dayrooms had newspapers and a radio. Female patients were encouraged in rug-making, and others were expected to turn the waste of the asylum into creative use – rags torn into fuel for the boilers, newspapers shredded to make stuffing for the bedding of the incontinent. Whenever possible, attendants would assist exercise in the airing courts.

Later, in 1933, the Board of Control issued a *Memorandum on Occupation Therapy for Mental Patients*. It recommended the appointment of a specialist occupational therapist, but Talgarth could not afford one and this remained the situation until after World War Two. The best that could be done was the appointment of a practically-minded male attendant who was paid an extra £5 per week for his work.

This, then, was the therapeutic treatment from which, optimistically, around one-third of the short-stay patients were expected to benefit, leading to their discharge. With only the Medical Superintendent and Assistant Medical Officer as fully trained practitioners on site, not much more could be attempted; nor was it expected, though the benefits of sympathetic counselling by individual attendants should not be forgotten.

There were drugs. The sedative Paraldehyde was given as an anti-convulsant and sleeping potion, and continued to be a staple drug at Talgarth up until the 1960s. Bromide was another sedative which was also supposed to curb the sex urge. Morphine dissolved in beer or vinegar was a last resort to calm mania and be beneficial to melancholics; its substitute, chloral hydrate, was used more often. And then there was, simply, a prolonged hot bath with a cold flannel pressed to the head. The combination was supposed to calm mania, though the dangers of giving a maniac a hot bath led to a later Deputy Superintendent issuing another set of rules.

Finally, there were lithium salts – and herein lies the strange claim to fame of the first Medical Superintendent, Dr Ernest Jones. When Dr Diggle became Medical Superintendent in 1948 he discovered in the dispensary a large half-empty can of lithium salts which, judged from the writing on the label, dated from the early years of the century. Lithium salts were supposedly first given as a treatment for bipolar disorder by John Cade in Australia in 1948, and it is now on the WHO's List of Essential Medicines, despite side-effects such as nausea, confusion, diarrhoea and vertigo. It has to be presumed, then, that patients at Brecknock and Radnorshire Asylum who suffered from severe depression benefited from lithium salts 40 years earlier. Dr Jones must have taken the prescription with him to the other side of the world when he became Inspector General of the Insane for the Colony of Victoria in Australia.

Dr Diggle destroyed the tin.

The Eighteenth Annual Report of the Committee of Visitors presented in 1921 makes no mention of treatment or, for that matter, discharges. It seems to assume that outdoor occupation was an end in itself:

> A very satisfactory number of both male and female patients have been usefully employed in the gardens, farm and laundry. All the year round a good proportion of patients went for walks inside and outside the asylum grounds.

MID·WALES HOSPITAL

Bathing Rules

1. Every patient is to be bathed immediately after admission unless the Medical Officer admitting the patient orders otherwise.

2. The name of every patient not having the customary Bath must be recorded in the Daily Report.

3. In preparing a bath THE COLD WATER MUST BE TURNED ON FIRST.

4. Before the patient enters the Bath, the temperature is to be ascertained by the Thermometer. The temperature must not exceed 98 degrees, or be less than 88 degrees. In case of the Thermometer becoming inefficient or broken, bathing to be suspended until another be obtained. THE NURSE MUST BE SURE BY TESTING HERSELF THAT THE WATER IS NOT TOO HOT OR TOO COLD.

5. A fresh supply of water is to be used for each Patient, and under no circumstances are two Patients to Occupy the Bath at the same time

6. During the employment of the Bath, the room is never to be left without a Nurse. At all other times the Bath waste is to be left open, and the Bathroom door to be kept locked.

7. UNDER NO PRETENCE WHATEVER IS THE PATIENT'S HEAD TO BE PUT UNDER WATER.

8. In the bath the body of each Patient is to be well cleansed with soap. After coming out of the Bath care must be taken to thoroughly dry the Patients, especially those who are feeble and helpless, and to clothe them as rapidly as possible.

9. The Bath Key is never to remain on the tap, and must never be trusted to a patient. When not in use to be locked up.

10. Any marks, bruises, wounds, sores, local pain, or evidence of Disease of any kind complained of by a Patient, or noticed by a Nurse, to be immediately reported, and also entered in the Daily Report.

11. Baths are only to be given for the purpose of cleanliness except on a Medical Officer's Orders.

12. No patient, under any circumstances, is to be given a cold bath.

13. Medicated Baths will be ordered by a Medical Officer when necessary. They must not be used otherwise.

14. IF IN ANY DOUBT AS TO WHETHER A PATIENT IS FIT FOR A BATH, DO NOT BATHE THE PATIENT UNTIL YOU HAVE HAD A MEDICAL OFFICER'S INSTRUCTIONS.

GORDON DIGGLE,
Medical Superintendent.

Dr Diggle's Bathing Rules

'Shell-shock' victims of the Great War

World War One arrived at the remote community of Talgarth the very same day that it was declared on 4 August 1914. At a meeting in the Town Hall, Lord Glanusk, who was Commanding Officer of the Brecon Territorials as well as being Chairman of the Committee that had built the asylum, called for a recruitment campaign and 20 young men instantly 'rushed to volunteer.' Only two days later, the 1st Brecknock Battalion marched off to Talgarth station behind a bugle band and was cheered away by a 'packed Talgarth'.

Within days, the new Assistant Medical Officer Peter Drummond asked the Visiting Committee for permission to enlist. It was granted. A few months later Dr Pugh himself asked permission and this was refused. The Hall Porter Albert Fawke felt it his duty to enlist, as a single man, and his application was accepted because he had had the foresight to obtain a replacement who was ineligible for military service. In November 1915 the Board of Control (which replaced the Commissioners in Lunacy) asked the Visiting Committee to assess the number of male attendants absolutely essential for maintaining the work of the asylum.

At about the same time, Dr Pugh told the Visiting Committee that the Recreation Hall could be used for the treatment of wounded soldiers. The Area Commander turned the offer down. He had chosen Cardiff Mental Hospital instead; therefore the Talgarth asylum had to find room for an extra 100 male patients and 35 female patients transferred from Cardiff. This led to overcrowding, with beds in the male wards jammed side by side. The result was that only a few members of staff and no attendants were allowed to enlist in future. The male staff was already depleted because so many young men from Talgarth and around had joined up.

Four former staff from the asylum were killed in the Great War. Their names are on a brass plaque now in Bronllys Hospital. Corporal Smith had been a gardener, Private Watkins a shepherd, Lance Corporal

Reed an attendant, and the fourth was Private Lloyd. Behind the chapel at Talgarth is a Commonwealth War Grave, commemorating Private John Lewis, aged 47, who may well have been a patient before the War.

Then, in March 1917, the Visiting Committee considered a letter from the Board of Control 'concerning the treatment in the asylum of discharged soldiers and sailors suffering from mental disorder'. This was the beginning of a new category of patient, the Service Patient, whose pension was paid by the War Office. 'Shell shock' was coming to Talgarth.

The military authorities disliked the term 'shell shock', preferring the vague 'neurasthenia' or 'nervous exhaustion', which downgraded the trauma, but the Tommies knew what it meant:

> Of course you've heard of shell shock,
> But I don't suppose you think,
> What a wreck it leaves a chap
> After being in the pink...
> Of course, you lose your speech, Sir,
> Perhaps you're deaf as well,
> But you don't get no gold stripe to show,
> Although you've fought and fell.

Shell shock affected far more soldiers than those who suffered from the explosion of shells. It stood for the psychological and emotional stress of war. Severe victims showed symptoms of nightmares, hallucination, insomnia, paralysis (including dumbness), hysteria, mental regression and severe depression. This was nothing to do with cowardice or shirking, as some of the Generals claimed, though interestingly there was less shell shock in regiments with a high morale.

In 1914 the Board of Control took over what became Moss Side Mental Hospital in Maghull near Liverpool and began an important evaluation. Over the next two years Maghull took in 748 Army patients who suffered the psychological and emotional stress of war. Eventually, 385 were discharged as fit for service again but 219 were retained; of these, 107 were classed as chronic lunatics and 18 as epileptics. Three implications are clear. The first is that war made some men insane but many shell-shock victims recovered after a peaceful life away from the War. The third implication is hard to accept: some enlisted soldiers were, in the language of the time, lunatics. As William Robinson, the Senior Assistant Medical Officer at the West Riding Asylum, wrote in 1921, many ex-servicemen left in asylums were 'feeble-minded lads, moral imbeciles and epileptics', who had been allowed into the Army because of poor medical screening. They might not have been recruited to fight at the Front but some had ended up there when manpower shortage was at its most acute. Later they were wrongly diagnosed as shell-shock cases. Presumably Talgarth had its share of these; this is hinted at in the Visiting Committee minutes of March 1918 which refer to 'the Service Class of soldiers and sailors disabled by mental unfitness certified as due to or aggravated by war service during the present war'.

The number of 'shell-shocked' ex-servicemen in the UK increased after the Armistice. In 1920 there were 63,296 in receipt of Army pensions, in 1925 there were 74,289 and in 1929 there were slightly more, fully 11 years after the end of the War. The numbers in Talgarth reflect this up to a point. Under the Mental Treatment Act of 1915 all soldiers suffering from shell shock had to be treated for six months before, if necessary, they could be certified and sent to an asylum. Consequently, some of those who entered Talgarth did not do so of their own free will. In May 1918, four 'Service Patients' were admitted, although one escaped and as he was 'not recaptured within the statutory period of 14 days' he was allowed to go free. (This challenge, if that is the right word, applied to all asylum patients.) Then, through 1919 and 1920, admissions averaged 3 per month with some soon discharged as 'not insane'. In 1921 many Service Patients at Brecknock and Radnor Asylum were transferred to Cardiff City Mental Hospital, 15 between January and March. Then the figures went down. Presumably Cardiff became the main recipient of shell-shocked soldiers in the area.

It would be wrong to suppose that all shell-shock victims in asylums were insane or mentally defective. There must have been some in the Brecknock and Radnor who were there because they needed institutional treatment and had nowhere else to go. After the war the Ex-Servicemen's Welfare Society was founded to campaign against the prejudice that 'neurasthenics' were lunatics; they deserved homes for heroes and not asylums. Realistically, the ESWS argued, badly shell-shocked men should be treated in mental wards attached to general hospitals or in special recuperative homes. It was the public consciousness that asylums were, once again, being used as dumping grounds that contributed to the change in name from 'asylum' to 'mental hospital'.

There is a disturbing postscript to this. As late as 1953 the Welsh Border Hospital Management Committee reported that there were still eight 'Great War Cases' remaining at Talgarth:

> They are of varying degrees of senility and increasing dementia, displaying every evidence of friendliness and happiness in their surroundings in so far as they are able to express any emotion.

From asylum to mental hospital

In April 1921 Montgomeryshire County Council joined with Brecon and Radnorshire Councils in sending patients to the asylum paid for out of the rates. From then on, patients were grouped on wards as far as possible according to their county and language, for many patients from Montgomery were Welsh-speakers; quite a number of the attendants also spoke Welsh, some of them having come from north Wales looking for work. From Welshpool to Talgarth is over 70 miles of largely remote country, from the soft landscape of patchwork fields and gentle hills of Montgomeryshire to the bleak Black Mountains. Many a patient must have been homesick; all too many rarely, if ever, received visits from home, perhaps because of the paucity of public transport. By the end of 1925 there were 455 patients, the majority female, and this meant more beds were needed. So Wards East 7 and East 8 were built to house 60 female patients. This was known as the New Block, located at the east end of the hospital grounds, beyond the mortuary.

In July 1920, King George V opened the South Wales Sanatorium at Bronllys, north of the main Hereford to Brecon road on the opposite side of Talgarth from the Mid Wales. Like the other 17 sanatoria in Wales, it was intended for sufferers from pulmonary TB, many of them miners whose lungs were clogged with coal dust. In its way it was as impressive a site as the Mid Wales hospital, covering 300 acres with farm and gardens. The 17 new buildings included 'pavilions' in which each patient had their own room leading onto a terrace so that the beds could be wheeled out into the fresh air. It soon was renamed Bronllys Hospital. Thus two major specialised hospitals existed within 3 miles of each other: this would have huge implications seventy years later.

Dr Pugh died in service on 12 April 1923. He was succeeded by the A.M.O. Peter Drummond, who had returned safely from the War. Dr Pugh died two years after his asylum had been renamed, for the amalgamation with Montgomeryshire was the pretext for a new name 'The Mid-Wales Counties Mental Hospital'. This anticipated the law, because the Mental Treatment Act of 1930 decreed that the term 'asylum' should no longer be used. The Act also officially replaced the old word 'lunatic' by 'patient', implying that mental illness was an illness like any other.

Nevertheless, throughout this period the Visiting Committee continued to complain about the senile and 'mental defectives' who were clogging up the Mid Wales Mental Hospital. The Annual Report of 1932:

'It should be in the interests of the Joint County Councils that patients suffering from Senile Decay should be treated in the Poor Law institutions instead of sending them to the Mental Hospital'. A Visiting Committee inspection of 1928:

> S. B. is a nice looking boy of 16 but of slow comprehension. He is working very well in the tailor's shop. Mr Drummond is of the opinion that he is a high grade mental defective and every effort should be made to get him to a M.D. institution. His father died here and his mother is a patient here. It would be a pity to send him back to the workhouse but this is not the best place for him.

A start was made in 1936 when Miss Avery Jones was appointed Boarding Out Officer. Her job was to find Guardians who, approved by the Mental Deficiency Committees of the County Councils, would be paid to look after such patients. This scheme also covered other patients who were discharged from the Mid Wales. Encouraged by the Mental Treatment Act of 1930, an Outpatients service was set up, with the power given to the Medical Superintendent to require specified attendance days for patients who had been discharged.

These, however, were only small measures to relieve the pressure on beds. The truth was that by the end of the 1930s mental hospitals everywhere were clogging up with incurable and institutionalised patients: the longer a patient was inside what sociologists call a 'total institution' the less chance he or she had of re-joining the community outside. Many of the elderly patients suffered from the mental illnesses of old age too, like dementia and Alzheimer's disease. The figures speak for themselves. At the Mid Wales every year there was a death rate between 8 and 9 per cent, that is 35 patients on the assumption that the total number of patients was 400. There was a discharge rate that was slightly higher, say

50 patients a year, either labelled as 'recovered' or 'relieved' which meant that they could very well find themselves back inside later. That amounts to a 'turnover' of roughly 20 per cent, with the average length of incarceration growing longer and longer. The Register of Deaths at the Mid Wales between 1930 and 1940 shows that over one third of the patients (37 per cent) who died during that decade had been in the Mid Wales for over ten years. That figure would rise.

It is a melancholy fact that behind and at the sides of the chapel at the Mid Wales hospital there are over 1,000 unmarked graves. The Register of Burials states this clearly under the heading: 'Burials in the chapel at Talgarth hospital. Graveyard undefined and graves appear to be Unmarked'. Between 1903 and 1965, 800 burials were recorded of patients between the ages of 17 and 97, of whom 68 were over 80. That is an average of 13 burials a year of patients whose families, presumably, had forgotten them or at least did not want to bury them. Apart from their fellow patients and the staff at the Mental Hospital they were alone and unloved. The catchment area of remote farms several hours' travel away by public transport – if there was any – contributed to the isolation and dependence. In the early days of the asylum there seem to have been more unclaimed bodies, too, because in 1920 the Visiting Committee resolved:

> … that unclaimed bodies of patients dying in the asylum be sent to the Medical Schools under the provision of the Anatomy Act and without a previous post mortem examination, at the discretion of the Medical Superintendent.

Burials close to the hospital chapel continued well into the 1980s, the graves being dug during the 1950s and 1960s by a long-term patient with the suitably biblical name of Absalom. He was known by all as 'Abby' and combined this job with being the self-appointed choir master. Many a time he would abscond from his ward, collect together other 'choristers', and be discovered in the chapel singing hymns.

There is one tombstone in the graveyard that may well mark the grave of a patient: 'In loving memory of GEORGE, son of James and S. A. Cook of Welshpool who died July 2nd 1922 aged 36 years'.

There is another marker too, a small marble block beneath a pine tree. Rumour has it that it marks the grave of a patient who was murdered by other patients; the spooky state of decay of the Mid Wales now encourages such rumours.

The spectre of schizophrenia

By the 1930s the optimism of Lord Glanusk about 'the speedy restoration to health' had been eroded into a sense of therapeutic pessimism that pervaded the asylum world. Too many patients in the asylums were incurable and the longer they were inside the longer they would have to stay. Then came the concept of schizophrenia. This was not new because it originated in Germany before Talgarth asylum had even been built, but it was not until the inter-war period that it impacted on asylums in Britain. Schizophrenia (literally a 'split mind') was not a new form of mental illness but a new diagnosis. It divided psychosis, that is the extreme mental disorder when thoughts and emotions lose touch with reality, into curable and incurable forms.

The curable form, cycled through distinct phases and often going into remission, was labelled 'manic-depression'; the incurable form, initially called *dementia praecox* but then the new diagnostic category of 'schizophrenia', was thought to be caused by degenerative brain disease and therefore incurable. These categories remain the basis of psychotic disorders today though the efficacy of treatment through drugs means that schizophrenia need not be incurable.

The symptoms of schizophrenia include hallucinations (particularly hearing voices), delusions, catatonic behaviour (dramatically reduced activity leading to stupor), incoherent speech often caused by thought disorder, and extreme paranoia. To be medically diagnosed as schizophrenic today requires the patient to exhibit two of these symptoms over a one-month period and the illness must cause severe social and occupational dysfunction. Schizophrenia does not mean a 'split personality', as in the sense of the Conan Doyle book *Jekyll and Hyde*, nor does it mean violent behaviour (at least compared to drug or alcohol abuse). About 8 per cent of schizophrenics with no other illness commit violent acts, but that figure rises to 30 per cent if it is combined with drug or alcohol abuse. Schizophrenia normally develops during youth and affects perhaps one person in 100 at some time. Many patients at Talgarth from the beginning were obviously schizophrenic, but it was not until the 1940s that the term appears in the records. Not that it made any difference to treatment, for schizophrenics were regarded as incurable and that spread further gloom through the asylum world.

Today schizophrenics are treated with drugs and psychiatric therapy like CBT (cognitive behaviour therapy) and many recover. Between the 1940s and 60s more drastic cures were attempted in mental hospitals including the Mid Wales; they are the subject of the later chapter 'Brave New World'.

Despite the grim history of the Mid Wales as an asylum, all the nurses I interviewed say what a caring place the hospital was in their lifetime. In a sense, they say, it was a happy extended family because many of the patients were lovable and supportive and the others seemed at least grateful. I wonder if it was any different in the earlier days of the asylum? There was plenty to encourage and divert the staff. A career was almost inevitable because the asylums promoted staff from within, and this was even more so at Talgarth because of its isolation. There was an active social life centred on the magnificent dining and recreation hall; dancing, dramatics and, as early as 1922, the arrival of silent movies were all hugely popular with the patients too. There was sport: cricket on a fine pitch drained by a clinker base deposited from the boilers, a snooker tournament for a silver cup donated by Dr Pugh. Then there were the market gardens where every attendant was allowed an allotment, and the services like tailoring and shoemaking which offered staff discounts. It was an extension of the community of Talgarth and popular within the town.

All this, however, was about to change in a way no one could have predicted.

Chapter Two
Camp 234

Bill Devereux grew up to spend his working life at the Mid Wales Hospital, ending as a senior Charge Nurse. He is one of several who remember their childhood encounters with prisoners of war around Talgarth:

> I was born in 4 Hospital Villas. My father was Head Storekeeper. In 1939, when I was four, the war started and soon after many of our patients with the nurses were taken to hospitals in Hereford, Denbigh and Carmarthen. In their place came soldiers: German and Italian prisoners of war, and psychiatric soldiers [shell shocked] from the British Army. So Nissen huts were built, a NAAFI and the NAAFI girls' sleeping quarters and the whole hospital was surrounded with 15-foot double barbed wire.
>
> My playmates were psychiatric patients, German and Italian prisoners of war and soldiers. Quite safe! They taught me how to poach, how to box, anything that wasn't academic.
>
> I can remember the Italian prisoners wearing brown uniform with large blue or red patches and they would call me to the barbed wire: 'Bambino, bambino, get us such and such from Talgarth'. When it was Red Cross Day, me and my brother Brian would take up a small biscuit tin and they would fill it with sweets. And we were quite ill smoking the cigarettes called Fifteens that came in a naval packet.

Gwyn Williams and his dad were driving along the remote track at Rhos Fach when a German captain with his armed escort appeared out of the mist and saluted. Others remember chasing after the lorry that picked up Italian POWs in the Market Place at Talgarth to take them to work on the farms and shouting 'Wops! Wops!', the rude nickname for Italians in those days. Roy Thomas of Gwernllwyd Farm just up the road from the Mid Wales remembers his father talking about the POWs who installed water pipes on his farm: 'the Germans were efficient and hard workers; the Italians were useless'. These are vivid memories, like dreams that don't go away.

How had this come about? How did the Mid Wales Joint Counties Mental Hospital, renamed in 1940 the Talgarth Military Hospital, become one of the nine hospitals for psychotic Allied servicemen and then, known as Camp 234, the only hospital in the United Kingdom for mentally ill prisoners of war from Germany and Italy?

Talgarth Military Hospital 1940–1947

'Shell shock' was a term commonly understood; Post-Traumatic Stress Disorder was a term not yet invented. The Army phraseology was far more careful than in the Great War. It used the term 'psychiatric casualty'. Americans referred to 'Combat Exhaustion'. It was the defeat of the British Expeditionary Force in northern France in the spring of 1940, resulting in the evacuation from Dunkirk, that first rang alarm bells in the Royal Army Medical Corps (RAMC).

Ten to fifteen per cent of the battle casualties during the Dunkirk campaign were psychiatric, the first acute cases that the British medical services had encountered in the war. Soon after, two doctors who worked at a special neurological hospital near London wrote an article for the authoritative medical magazine *The Lancet* entitled 'Acute War Neuroses' (by Clifford Allen and Millais Culpin) about the soldier patients they had treated. They reported that most of the Dunkirk survivors who had become patients looked similar: signs of physical exhaustion, thin 'fallen-in' faces with pallid complexions. Their whole attitude indicated tension, anxiety or listless apathy. Many had uncontrollable tremors, like patients with Parkinson's. Mentally, they were troubled by sleeplessness and terrifying dreams; they were startled by the slightest noise. Some suffered from amnesia (loss of memory) and various kinds of hysteria.

Dunkirk, it appeared, had caused its own kind of breakdown on top of the cumulative strains of war. These soldier patients had retreated continuously for weeks with little possibility of fighting back. They resented the bad leadership and inferior equipment. They felt guilty of failure:

> Their army had retreated, their ships bombed, and their country itself was threatened. Their neurotic demands could not be satisfied: they were dependent children who could not forget the injury done to them. They said 'I am ill and weak and cannot serve' but what they meant was 'I can find security only at home and even there no-one will protect me from myself'.

The immediate treatment, the article went on, was rest, regular meals and narcotic (sleep inducing) drugs, followed by psychotherapy. Most of the patients reported back for duty but were still troubled by physical exhaustion, nightmares and anxiety. The article concluded 'if a man firmly believes he will break down in a particular way in particular circumstances, and he has already done so once, then he will do so again'.

Alarm bells led to action. Army psychiatrists were appointed to each Command and, to quote from the official *Notes on the Administration of Army Psychiatry 1939–1943,* a crucial decision was taken:

> The peacetime policy of discharging immediately to civil care all soldiers who became 'insane' was applied in 1914–1918. It aroused considerable protest from the public [because too often the soldiers ended up in asylums]. In 1940 it was decided to treat such cases in the Service as far as possible.

The period in military hospitals would enable proper diagnosis to be made, active treatment to be given, short psychotic episodes to recover and the question of attributability [*sic*] to be explored carefully.

There is an important advantage in converting a portion of a civilian hospital into a separate military hospital. It means that military patients may be admitted without certification. The Superintendent of the civilian hospital shall be given an unpaid commission in the RAMC and act as Officer Commanding while continuing his duties in respect of the civilian institution.

So the War Office took over nine civilian hospitals for psychotic Service patients and one of these was the Mid Wales Mental Hospital at Talgarth, henceforth known as the Talgarth Military Hospital. It served the Western Command and opened on 18 October 1940. The Medical Superintendent of the Mid Wales, Peter Drummond, who had served in the Great War, was appointed Lieutenant Colonel.

In 1942 a Directorate of Army Psychiatry was established with 227 army psychiatrists serving, 97 of them abroad in areas of conflict. Military psychiatry had come of age. The Directorate insisted that, compared to the Great War, far greater care should be taken at enlistment to recognise mental unsuitability; and greater care should be taken during army service to monitor mental instability. It defined the three psychiatric categories that made up the official definition of shell shock as 'a man who becomes ineffective in battle as a direct result of his personality being unable to stand up to the stresses of combat'.

The first category was 'psychosis': that is, the abnormal condition of the mind that involves a loss of contact with reality, leading to aberrant behaviour resulting at its most severe in schizophrenia. In former times this was known as 'insanity' and it was for these soldiers, made 'insane' by war, that Talgarth was intended.

The second category was 'psycho-neurosis' (the term 'anxiety-neurosis' would be used today), meaning that the soldier's nerves had temporarily broken down because of battle stress, leading to extreme anxiety, lack of self-control and so on. This term was equivalent to the 'neurasthenic' label given to shell-shocked soldiers in the Great War and was often an attempt to downgrade the severity of the psychiatric disorder. For these soldiers, as with civilians suffering as a result of German bombing, EMS (Emergency Medical Services) Neurosis Centres were more appropriate than hospitals. The Directorate began a scheme where an army psychiatrist could recommend a return to the army for such cases, but not to combat areas.

The third category was 'mental defect'. 'Mental defectives' could now be discharged from the Army by a psychiatrist without a medical board. 'The problem of dullness and backwardness in the army has proved exceptionally large', said the *Notes on Army Psychiatry 1939–1943*. 'About 8 per cent of all Army intake are unsuitable to bear arms'. They were often transferred to the Pioneer Corps which was 'notably successful in utilising thousands of dullards who are quite incapable of military training'. It was the Pioneer Corps, carrying rifles, who guarded the POWs at Talgarth.

Army psychiatrists also recognized a form of psychosomatic illness, that is an illness caused by psychological factors rather than physical. Soldiers who doubted their courage and feared the shame of cowardice sometimes developed disorders like digestive complaints, intractable skin diseases or erratic heartbeats. There were, apparently, thousands who were discharged from the Army with these complaints before they ever went into battle.

The first discussions about a military takeover of the Mid Wales Mental Hospital had occurred at the Visiting Committee meeting on 13 July 1940. The Board of Control had passed on the request from the War Office 'to convert a large part of the hospital into a military hospital'. In the summer of 1940, when the common assumption was that Nazi Germany could invade at any moment, it was not the sort of request that could be turned down. Yet the Mid Wales Mental Hospital had some patients that could not be moved and new arrivals who would always need to be treated there. The compromise was reached that 'the military' would take over 315 beds while a hundred or so civilian patients would remain. So 320 patients were transferred; 143 were sent to the mental hospital in Hereford, 113 to Carmarthen and 64 to Denbigh, accompanied by nurses. According to the Visiting Committee Report for 1941, a high number of deaths occurred as a result of this transfer: 8 in Talgarth at the anticipation of being moved and 54 in the 'Receiving Hospitals', extraordinary proof how unsettling a change of institution must be to the severely mentally disturbed. Presumably neither staff nor patients had any say in the matter. Two-thirds of the staff accommodation was given up, eventually, to house 75 army nurses and administrative staff from the RAMC and QAIMNS (Queen Alexandra's Imperial Military Nursing Service). In 1943, accommodation was provided for them in Nissen huts built in the 'airing courts' attached to the male wards.

Sir Hubert Bond of the Board of Control assured the Visiting Committee that the hospital would be handed back at the end of the war 'in excellent condition'. He assured the Committee that it would keep control of the civilian hospital that remained. Moreover, the War Office was generous with compensation. It made a down payment of £25,000, with another £1,550 to the farm for food and more to local suppliers. It paid for the 'removal of patients' and 'the transfer of staff'. Mindful of the unpopular decision to uproot staff for the duration of the war, the War Office offered to pay travelling expenses for trips home and even a double rent for transferred married male staff – one for the family remaining in Talgarth and the other at the Receiving Hospitals. The War Office confirmed that the new Lt Col. Drummond would be in overall charge; so the deal was done.

Lt Col. Drummond's War Diary is kept in the Public Records at Kew. The War Diary was an official requirement for each service unit to fill in weekly to give an accurate account of operations for future historians.

They are dry accounts kept to a minimum, which is not surprising considering the circumstances. Drummond's are no exception. They do not recount the human side, such as what the British soldiers did or how they related to the mentally ill prisoners of war who began to arrive at Talgarth in increasing numbers once the British Army went on the offensive, first in North Africa, then in Italy, and then after D-Day in northern Europe.

Drummond's first entry is for April 1941, which suggests that several months had been needed after the transfer to the War Office for the military wards to become operational. He is most concerned to record the numbers of armed forces patients admitted and discharged every month. Dry though these statistics are, a lot may be read into them. For example, in February 1942:

> 58 patients were admitted: 46 from the Regular Army, 3 from the Royal Air Force, 1 from the Royal Norwegian Navy, 3 Czech troops and 5 Prisoners of War (4 Italian and 1 German).
>
> The same month 64 patients were discharged. Of these 46 were from the Regular Army: 40 of these were put in the care of relatives after they had been discharged from the Army as unfit for any further form of military service, 4 returned to unit and 2 were discharged to Public Assistance Institutions. 5 were from the Royal Navy, all transferred to the Royal Naval Auxiliary Hospital at Fareham. 9 were discharged from the Royal Air Force to the care of relatives as permanently unfit for any form of service and 1 was returned to duty. 1 from the Free French Forces and 2 from the Czech Forces were returned to duty.

Nearly two years later, in December 1943, the numbers looked like this:

> 115 patients were admitted: 56 were from the British Army, 51 directly from overseas and 5 were repatriated from Germany (presumably captives from POW camps there). 13 were from the RAF, 10 from the Royal Navy, 5 from other Allied Forces and 31 Prisoners of War (Italian).
>
> 37 patients were discharged. 17 of these were from the British Army of whom 1 was returned to unit, 9 sent to relatives after discharge from Army, and 7 sent to civilian mental hospitals or other hospitals. 1 RAF patient was discharged and sent to relatives and 1 Royal Navy likewise.
>
> 15 Italian POWs were transferred to P/W (Prisoner of War) camps.

What may be deduced from this? The first deduction is that Talgarth was fulfilling its function of a hospital where 'a proper diagnosis may be made', and after this it seems to have served as a clearing station from which as many patients as possible were discharged. When a Medical Board recommended that the patient was permanently unfit for the Armed Forces, he was sent home as soon as possible. Presumably, he was still psychotic or 'psycho-neurotic' or else he would not have been judged permanently unfit for further service, but now he was, in most cases, dumped on his family. This was in accord with policy, because an Army Order of September 1942 ruled that nine months was the maximum time for psychotic patients to be treated in military hospitals and, after three months, duty pay would stop. (This was not the case with mentally ill POWs, as we shall see.)

The second deduction is that using Talgarth as a clearing hospital was an administrative nightmare. Drummond frequently complained about this: 'Deficiencies in establishment curtail treatment, supervision, recreation and discharge of patients. This has been represented to the higher authorities on several occasions'. Staff hours required per week went up from 60 to 78 (including meal times), which meant at least a ten-hour day. It was all too much for the Matron, Miss Lawrence (did she have a military rank?), who resigned on health grounds in May 1944, suffering from 'a neurotic condition with anxiety symptoms and considerable emotional instability' (Visiting Committee Minutes). The cooks were run ragged. There were only four of them and they were required to produce 635 meal portions twice a day: for 315 military patients plus 14 officers and 128 other ranks and 138 civilian patients plus 40 staff.

The British and Allied service patients wore blue uniforms with red ties. Those who were up and about played a lot of cricket and football, strolled around the grounds and attended occupational therapy. A daily drill took place in the Recreation Hall for all able-bodied patients, British, Allied and POWs together: it must have required all the disciplinary force of the proverbial Sergeant Major who conducted it. The British and Allied patients may well have visited the shops and pubs in Talgarth, but there is no record of this. The treatment provided was mostly sedative drugs and quiet recuperation. There was no psychiatric treatment offered at Talgarth, but in April 1942 the first 'electrical apparatus for Convulsive Therapy' was purchased. This MacPhail-Strauss Unit, costing £50, was used frequently with controversial results (see below).

As the war moved from defence of the Home Front on to the offensive in Europe, so the proportion of British and Allied service patients went down and that of POWs went up. By 1 December 1946, over a year after the war had ended, the War Office formally released a substantial part of its accommodation at Talgarth, reducing the number of military beds from 315 to 125. By this time these beds were almost entirely occupied by POW patients. Of course, as the Allied action in Europe gathered momentum, so more German and Italian soldiers, sailors and airmen were captured. But this does not explain why the numbers of British military mental casualties at Talgarth declined: the answer, probably, was due to a change of attitude in the Directorate of Army Psychiatry.

By 1944 the view was that psychiatric casualties had to be taken for granted – as inevitable a medical emergency as gunshot or shrapnel wounds – and most cases were more conveniently treated behind the lines in war zones, rather than at hospitals back in the UK. The treatment basically consisted of prolonged rest, good food and sedative drugs. Important, too, was the assurance that the condition was only temporary and not a form of physical illness. The Americans went so far as to replace the term 'war neurosis' by 'battle fatigue' which was normal after too much time in action. Most soldiers, said the US Army, reached their peak of effectiveness after 90 days and were 'ineffective after 140 days'. The heavy use of barbiturates and 'R and R' (rest and recuperation) were sufficient for 60 per cent of 'battle fatigue' casualties to be judged fit for return to the war.

This more casual attitude seems to have worked. An article in *The Lancet* titled *Psychiatric Casualties from the Normandy Beach Head* written a few months after D-Day in 1944 by three frontline psychiatrists, Charles Anderson, Mandred Jeffrey and N.Pai, reported that 10 per cent of the casualties of the first few days after D-Day had been psychiatric. Of these, 12 per cent had been unable to speak, 15 per cent had developed a stammer and 70 per cent had habitual nightmares, all symptoms of psycho-neurosis. Nevertheless, in contrast to the psychiatric casualties at Dunkirk (and in World War One for that matter), their morale was high, they did not feel a sense of shame and their ongoing treatment behind the lines had been prompt. 'As a result of treatment the majority had their neurosis arrested so that it did not develop into a more serious psychological disorder' said *The Lancet*. After complete rest and sedation most cases were returned to their units.

Presumably, it was too early to write whether they returned to the fighting and what symptoms of stress they continued to experience. In fact, post-war research would show that this claim by army psychiatrists that recuperation and return to action was possible in the majority of cases was very optimistic (an attempt, some thought, to improve the low status of psychiatrists in the army). Many soldiers relapsed and many served only in the rear. However, these were the statistics that shaped policy then.

At the same time, specialist hospitals for severe psychiatric cases were being set up in the UK, the largest of which was Hollymoor, near Birmingham. Here group therapy was pioneered as a major part of psychological rehabilitation. Talgarth was not one of these specialist hospitals. According to Drummond's War Diary, on 23 November 1944 he received instruction from the War Office not to accommodate more British psychotic cases for the time being at Talgarth; many of the remainder were sent to the Military Hospital at Ashurst, near Oxford.

That was not the end of the matter because, as in the Great War, the number of psychotic or 'psycho-neurotic' cases did not decrease at the War's end. In 1945 Talgarth was called on to take more military patients. At the same time, soldiers of the RAMC were being demobbed, so the War Office proposed to replace them by civilian staff. Once again, the Visiting Committee complained; once again, it was bought off, this time by the offer of an additional medical officer who would serve both military and civilian wards and be paid for by the army. It was not until near the end of 1946 that the War Office gave up most of its military establishment at Talgarth, but that left 125 mentally ill prisoners of war. By this time the War Office had brought in the Red Cross and the Order of St John in a Joint War Organisation to run what was left of the Military Hospital.

Camp 234

Talgarth Military Hospital was designated Camp 234 for prisoners of war, the only hospital in the U.K. for prisoners of war who were psychotic or 'psycho-neurotic', in part because of their war experiences. German Johannes G— was one:

Navy U Boat section. Johannes G——— suffers from schizophrenia. He was taken prisoner in July 1943 after rescue from a rubber dinghy and admitted to Talgarth with paranoid schizophrenia. He is depressed, sleepless, suspicious of everyone in camp. At times he is agitated and emotional. Needs to be on closed ward. Accepted for repatriation.

Shortly afterwards he committed suicide.

Otto S——— was another:

He has post-concussion syndrome, headaches, blackouts and insomnia after crash landing at 200 mph in April 1943. He was sent to Chepstow and then on to Talgarth with severe anxiety and hyper-venting behaviour. Almost wholly psycho-neurotic and depressive. Unlikely to recover while a POW. Does not require detention in psychosis hospital. Accepted for repatriation.

These two reports come from the papers and diaries of Dr Hugo Rast, a Swiss general surgeon working at the German Hospital in London. In January 1941 he was appointed President of the Mixed Medical Commission that was tasked with visiting all the POW hospitals to assess which patients should be repatriated home. His diaries provide a detailed insider view of what was going on at Camp 234 between 1942–1943. It is a remarkable archive that is kept in the Rare Materials collection of the Wellcome Library in London; I doubt if its contents have been revealed before.

First, however, an overview. It must come as a surprise to know that during World War Two some 3.5 million Germans became prisoners of war of the British alone. In March 1941 when Britain was near defeat there were only 550 in the UK, mostly from the German merchant navy, submarines and the Luftwaffe (air force). Then, after the victory in North Africa (1943) and the advance through northern Europe following the D-

Day landings (1944), the numbers of German POWs quickly rose. The peak number of prisoners in the UK was 402,000 and this was in September 1946, over a year after the war ended. Some of the 3.5 million had been shipped to Canada or the United States, but the bulk of them were in Allied-controlled parts of Europe like France, Holland and later Germany itself. The reason so many were still prisoners in the UK after the war was over was firstly because conditions were so chaotic in dismembered Germany that they had nowhere to go and secondly because the UK was in desperate need of manual labour on the land and in industry. Over a quarter of a million captured Germans were earning their keep in this way in May 1946.

Italian POWs arrived earlier and left earlier, apart from those who chose to stay in the UK. Between 1941 and 1946 over 150,000 Italian prisoners were over here, kept in camps but mostly working on the land. Many had arrived after the Italian defeats in North Africa in 1941–42; when Italy surrendered in September 1943 they were given the choice of either co-operating or not co-operating. Those who cooperated were moved out of the camps and lived on the land as paid labourers; the rest remained prisoners of war. Most Italians had been repatriated by 1946 but 1,500 or so remained as civilians in Britain, many of them making their home here.

There were over 400 prisoner of war camps, mostly in agricultural areas and away from security risk; 80 per cent of them were in England. The archetypal building was the tunnel-shaped Nissen hut fabricated from sheets of corrugated iron bolted together. This served variously as bunkhouse, canteen, storeroom, library; the site was surrounded by barbed wire and patrolled by guards from the Pioneer Corps. The POWs who lived in the camps were classified as low security risk, that is 'white' or 'grey'. POWs destined for South Wales arrived at Abergavenny General Processing Centre for classification before being sent to one of several camps in the area, each with its own number; Claremont Camp (29), Mardy Camp (118), Llanmartin Camp (184), The Mount Camp at

Chepstow (197), Llanover Park Camp (200) and the POW hospital at Chepstow (99).

Hardcore Nazis and members of the SS were given a 'black' classification and guarded elsewhere. All POWs were forced to watch film shot by the British Army when it entered Belsen concentration camp at the end of the War. Some SS refused to believe it, claiming that Belsen was a British camp in occupied Germany. As further evidence of twisted logic, some wounded SS POWs who required operations apparently refused general anaesthesia because they were told the British medics were planning to kill them.

Llanover Park, where the parks and gardens are now open to the public, had been used as a US Army camp before the D-day landings. After June 1944 it housed German and Italian POWs who worked on the land. One of them, the German Egon Schormann aged 23, wrote home on 22 September 1946 with a letter containing surprisingly specific statistics about camp life:

My dear ones,

This camp is called Llanover Park. There is nothing to be seen but barbed wire. The countryside is glorious. South Wales. But scenery is not enough for us. As soon as the food improves I shall start working again. With what we get here, I could just as well die of hunger in Germany. We have become ungrateful and we are, in any case, irritable. Our day begins at 7 and ends at 22.30. According to POW statistics I have written 1700 sides of paper and read 268 books [since early 1945 when he was captured in Holland]. We can write five letters and three cards per month.

Cases of divorce in our ranks are increasing. It is quite simple: the woman gets pregnant and then writes: 'Prepare yourself for a shock. I've had a bit of bad luck.' It is a terrible day for the husbands. Only yesterday they were still building their dreams on the loyalty of their wives and now they are holding letters like this in their hands. Captivity is a small school of life.

Young Egon was still a romantic who pined for his lover:

Lament
If only I could say your name just once,
And hold your hands in mine and touch your face,
And if I could ask Heaven when I'll be home –
How easy things would be – but still I can't.

If only I could get some news of you –
A little greeting breaking through the dark,
If I could know your heart still beats for me
How happy would I be – but I don't know.

Do you count up the hours, the days, the years –
Do you count time? Then prove your vision now!
Do you hold fast the only thing that's real –
Our Youth? – Oh no, you cannot hold it now.

Camp 99, the POW hospital in Chepstow, was frequently visited by Dr Rast on his way to Talgarth. On one occasion, he and his Mixed Medical Commission visited to assess, as usual, which cases should be recommended for repatriation. As at Talgarth, their preference was to send the prisoner patients home, partly because they were a drain on the taxpayer and partly because, provided they were not a security risk nor likely to fight again, they were using up beds. On the other hand, some were too ill to move. This visit, recorded in his diary, was just after the opening of Operation Overlord, the Allied invasion of northern Europe:

Christmas card to a nursing sister from German POWs in Camp 198,
Bridgend, Glamorgan; 1945.

Guard will not let us go straight in. He can – as usual – hardly read our passes, but insists not to let us pass the barbed wire entrance without further inspection. 2 fences of barbed wire round the hospital, with pathway for guards in between. Inner fence of rolled-up barbed wire.

The Medical Officer is a most pleasant Lt Col. youngish, a medical man. The service for examining the prisoners is this time perfect, without a hitch. All Germans appear in gala-uniform, grey-blue etc. with medals and ribbons, a great contrast to the slovenly Italians. They click heels and stretch out the right hand in the Nazi salute (but not all). In fact, their behaviour is more docile. Their morale has declined because of the impending defeat of Germany and loss of family at home. In 1940 there was an excited rush towards radios to hear of Axis successes, but now the radio is disregarded as 'BBC propaganda'.

Captain Blake [the War Office representative on the MMC] thinks there are a maximum of half a dozen German doctors among the prisoners in Britain. At Chepstow they try and get an Italian doctor to help. There are 270 beds here of which 238 are occupied; 84 by surgical cases, 72 by medical cases, 10 dysentery, and 20 venereal disease.

A few months later, Dr Rast visited again and made an inventory of the German prisoner patients applying for repatriation. It is interesting to note their youth:

167 POWs applied for repatriation, 92 nominated by the British Medical officer, 23 by the Camp Leader and 35 by the MMC. 42 were under 20, 53 between 20 and 25 and only 12 over 40. Most had been picked up after the invasion of Normandy and the drive into Germany.

15 suffered from head wounds, 45 from arm wounds, 30 from body wounds of whom 10 were paraplegic and 37 had received leg amputations with a further 28 severe fractures.

And so to Camp 234 at Talgarth. Dr Rast had made his first visit at the end of February 1942, on this occasion arriving from the north:

The weather has changed. It's drizzling and warmer. We move off by car at 9 a.m. through Chester towards Wrexham... After Newtown the road leads upwards, among beautiful hills and a soft landscape. The top of the pass has been ploughed for the first time in the national effort. The steep slopes are laid bare, all the young and old fir trees being felled. People on horseback. Sheep everywhere. Llandrindod Wells, with empty hotels, a kind of minor Tunbridge Wells. Road down a valley along a picturesque fishing river. Sheep and sheep again.

Talgarth our aim: military mental hospital; about 315 inmates from all three forces. The Hospital is tucked away on the hillslope, has a cricket pitch, is very isolated from the rest of the world; only two trains a day and no cinema. The local population is rather hostile towards a mental hospital.

There is a Lt Colonel Commandant [Drummond], 2 [doctor] Captains and 1 Lieutenant. One of them tells me that from the British Air Force they have only members of ground staff, never pilots [as patients]. British admissions include a good many conscientious objectors who later show signs of mental disorders.

We go and see 10 patients: 3 are German, all schizophrenic; 7 Italians, 1 congenital imbecile and the remainder schizophrenic. All 10 are A [the top classification for repatriation]. A doctor tells me he believes much in Cardiazol for excited patients [a drug that induced convulsions as a shock treatment for severe depressives; see next chapter], more still in the MacPhail-Strauss Convulsant Therapy Unit [ECT]. Blake does not know the disease and calls it 'Schaizophrinia'.

Incidentally, one of these 'doctor Captains' must have been Major Amedeo (Adam) Limentani, an Italian who served at Camp 234 with the RAMC. He later became a most distinguished psychoanalyst, and ultimately President of the British then the International Psychoanalytical Association. As a complete coincidence, Dr Michael Hession of the Mid Wales underwent psychoanalysis with him as part of his training.

In October Dr Rast was back again. This time he arrived at Newport by train and was driven to Talgarth in an army car. His ATS driver got lost on the way, which perhaps put Dr Rast out of humour:

The M.S. [Medical Superintendent] not very welcoming; leaves visit and does not offer tea. The Asylum looks dreary, empty, desolate, unfriendly. Rooms all cold, unheated. Same two Captain Medical Officers. This time they have lost their belief in electric shock treatment which they praised so much during our last visit. It is of no avail in schizophrenia. Visit patients from 3.45–5.15. 1 German and 12 Italians, 2 of whom we found to be normal. The other Italians brag about their disease, play act, go through the whole scale of apparent physical illnesses which they insist they are suffering from. 3/4 are hysterical. 1 Italian was an inmate of Benghazi Lunatic Asylum which was captured by the British in Feb 1941. We gave all an A for repatriation.

We are driven back to Chepstow where we stay in the George Hotel. Why is it that all the Inns in this country are

'Lions', mostly 'Red Lions', occasionally 'White Lions', even 'Golden Lions'?

On 2 March 1943, Dr Rast paid a fourth visit to 'Talgarth Military Lunatic Asylum' and this time he had a lot to write about, perhaps because he had an 'excellent local driver' to put him in a more responsive mood:

> Abergavenny. Mist hides hilltops. Hazel catkins all out. Country looks very bare. Long military convoys encountered all the way. Gurkhas at Brecon. Sheep in meadows and on road, many new born lambs.
>
> Arrived at Talgarth at 2.30. At present there are 100 prisoner patients, 96 Italians and 4 Germans. One escaped this morning and is still at large. Question: 'Should the guards shoot at them'? Our reply, 'NO as they are patients'.
>
> Italians show a lot of mass hysteria. When there is an incident on the ward they all become hysterical, throw themselves on the floor, perform cartwheels etc. The majority are real psychotics now. Many paranoid. They often fight among each other, e.g. North Italians against Southerners. 1 Italian jumped out of a window the other day to commit suicide but did not succeed.

There was no ambulance available at Talgarth until August 1944, when one was procured and the two lady drivers billeted locally. According to Drummond's War Diary, there were one or two attacks on guards during this time and several deaths or suicides, the deceased buried in Talgarth or Bronllys churchyards. Bill Devereux, who spent his childhood living next to the Hospital, remembers some German burials in the hospital grounds, the coffins draped with the German flag. In the 1950s, he says, the remains were disinterred for reburial in Germany.

Dr Rast continued his diary entry for March 1943:

Captivity may be a contributory factor to mental derangement. Is there such a thing as barbed wire psychosis? The C.O. [Drummond] remarks 'Most mental prisoners would definitely benefit from repatriation. Could this take place soon?' We reply 'The War Office decides, the MMC only proposes'.

Before entering a ward, we pass an enormous Drill Hall with stage etc. There, British, Italian and German prisoners are undergoing drill, altogether, and marched around by a drill master (Brit. Sergeant).

Talgarth has 315 beds. 2 wards are now used as barracks and 1 for clerks and personnel. It is a bare, dreary, dismal place, a labyrinth with long corridors where one always gets lost. In a bedded ward and its adjoining day room (with about 6 'cells' off), the Brit guards have rifles (unloaded I'm told) swung about their backs. The C.O. says the rifles are only a show of force. Every ward is run by a Sister. The orderlies are male, military.

The mental patients we saw today all appeared in brown battledress with blue or yellow patches. They were mostly a dull, sullen lot. Italians got up when we entered, mostly giving a Fascist salute.

At 5.10 pm we leave Talgarth by car, along big estates surrounded by stone walls. Pillboxes frequent at road crossings, on bridges and under trees in orchards. Old cathedral at Tintern. Beautiful scenery with river, hills, along valleys via Monmouth to Chepstow.

The last visit Dr Rast recorded in his diary was on 17 June 1943. Like any good doctor he is depressed about the effects on the mind of this kind of captivity and the lack of healing evident. His underlining shows his strength of feeling:

> The weather is beautiful. On the way from Abergavenny we pass whole slopes purple with flowering Digitalis.
>   The C.O., Lt Col. Drummond, makes himself scarce. The other day prisoner No. 82, a schizophrenic, tried to stab him but was found 'unfit to plead' at a Court martial. The British guards, we are told, are not reliable and want looking after themselves. They lose their keys and don't go after escaping patients.
>   There is one officer here (from Malta?) who speaks Italian and acts as interpreter. He says most POWs work in the garden and behave well. When repatriated home there is no trouble. The wireless is on the whole time in the wards, but the Italians think the broadcasts from London are propaganda because the bombing of Italian towns is reported and such news, they think, cannot be true.
>   <u>Electric shock therapy is a disappointment</u>. It is only good in depression and some cases of hysteria, esp. hysterical mutism. It is never properly monitored. As <u>sedatives</u>, patients are given Paraldehyde and also Chloral [Hydrate].
>   There are only 2 Germans here but 140 Italians. The Germans, of course, are spick and span. Many of the Italians are unshaven, which upsets Col. Blake [he must have been promoted].
>   62 per cent of the patients are suffering from schizophrenia and 17 per cent from manic depressive insanity. Persecutory ideas and depression are predominant. Suicide attempts are fairly common and a few homicidal attacks on other patients. Attempted escapes are common too. Most of these mental diseases began or manifested

themselves in captivity in England so the symptoms are only a few months old. The C.O. [Drummond] says 'Once a patient has been at Talgarth and is eventually sent to a Camp, he will always come back here again. Talgarth remains like a stain on those who have been here'.

Sex plays a considerable role with Italians. Idea that wife is unfaithful or such and such a patient is homosexual or impotent.

The psychopaths are mostly unstable, emotional and anti-social. They are conspicuous for the number of medals for gallantry which they wear.

Many of the schizophrenics are in grand form, full of delusions and hallucinations. One demands the first plane to fly to Italy; another is possessed by the devil; another, who is also mentally deficient, walks about naked and made a theatrical attempt to hang himself.

Nearly all are simple and illiterate and find hysteria the best way of expressing their emotions. I have to mention it again. Practically all the manifestations of mental disease began after captivity.

[This is not borne out by the case records that I have quoted earlier.]

5.30 pm. In beautiful weather down the Valley to Abergavenny where we stay at the Angel Hotel – good, with good food. I go for a walk and look in the beautiful evening sun across the plain and the valley of the Usk to the hills. Lovely.

The next day we pay our respects to the Military Commander in Wales, Major General Halstead (9 decorations). He says the Talgarth prisoners are a nuisance [presumably these are Italian POWs working on farms, rather than POW patients in camp 234]. The civil population resent them being well treated. The Italians flirt with the local women who – he says – funnily enough don't seem to mind at all. Passing bus drivers used to 'chip' [pretend to drive at?] the Italians; the Italians resented it and stoned the buses the next day. The General has received a petition from the Italians a) to prevent the local people jeering at them and b) to allow them to build their own sports ground.

The truth, as Lt Colonel Drummond proved by his War Diary, was that Camp 234 was little more than a holding area for POW patients in the same way that Talgarth Military Hospital was for Allied soldier patients. They were repatriated as soon as possible; this must have made those who remained feel insecure. In these circumstances treatment could only be rudimentary. Drummond's diary records that, in February 1944, 171 POWs were repatriated; in July '145 Italians entrained at Talgarth and 12 stretcher cases joined an ambulance at Hereford'; in October a further 71 Italians were repatriated, and so on. After September 1945 even Drummond had stopped counting: 'September–December 1945, large numbers of German POWs and Italians were repatriated'.

The truth about Rudolf Hess
Rudolf Hess, Hitler's Deputy Führer, flew to Scotland in May 1941 on his own initiative in order to arrange peace talks. Subsequently, the British considered him mentally ill. The rumour persists in Talgarth to this day that Hess spent some of his war years as a POW in Camp 234. Here is the true story, beginning with an entry in Dr Rast's diary.

Tuesday May 13th [1941].
Great news this morning. The Führer's Deputy Hess landed on Saturday in Scotland. Everybody and every patient is

Deputy Führer Rudolf Hess, Talgarth's secret patient

intrigued about this chap's reason for coming over here. He took a Messerschmitt from Augsburg and landed by parachute with a broken ankle this last Saturday during the great air raid on London. Hess is the topic of conversation everywhere.

Hess was taken to Mytchett Place in Surrey, a fortified mansion known as Camp Z where he stayed for over a year guarded by no fewer than 150 soldiers. Given the codename 'Jonathan', he was extensively debriefed by MI6 German experts. Had he been sent by Hitler? What did he know about Nazi war plans and the German military potential? Hitler, for his part, declared that Hess was mad, that he did not have any knowledge of his flight and that herewith he abolished the post of Deputy Führer. The psychiatrists who treated Hess did not find him insane but they did find him mentally unstable, given to paranoia and hypochondria.

Hess was visited frequently by Walther Thurnheer, the Swiss Chargé d'affaires in London who, as the representative of a neutral country, acted as the go-between for Hess and the British Government. On a visit in April 1942 he found Hess in bed, suffering from 'stomach cramps' because 'everyone was trying to poison him or rob him of his memory'. Hess went on to say that 'doors were banged 123 times in 30 minutes, that his sleep was disturbed by continuous coughing fits from the orderlies, but that he was sure the continuous noise would stop if he consumed a poisonous meal'. They then spent time wrapping and labelling food samples that Hess had secreted away convinced that analysis would reveal a well-known Mexican poison. Hess had already attempted suicide on more than one occasion.

By this time the Foreign Office and MI6 had concluded that Hess's venture had been a mad escapade on his own and that the German Government had no knowledge of it beforehand. Further, they had got little information out of Hess and were unlikely to get any more. While the propaganda value from Hess's flight was now exhausted, he should obviously not be allowed back to Germany. The question was where to put him for the duration of the War? Camp Z, near Aldershot, was a security risk and, given that it required a battalion of soldiers to protect it, highly expensive. So the War Office sent a representative to Talgarth Military Hospital in 'isolated South Wales' and he recommended that Hess should be sent there. But there was a problem. Colonel Bedford of the RAMC who briefed the War Office reported:

As it has been ruled that Z ['Jonathan'] is a Prisoner of War, there would appear to be no doubt that a Mixed Medical Commission would pass him as eligible for repatriation. If he were moved to an asylum, in his saner moments he would realise his position and demand examination by the MMC.

So Rudolf Hess ended the War years in Maindiff Court, a small hospital in a secluded position near Abergavenny. In peacetime it was attached to the County Mental Hospital but it had been taken over as a War Emergency Hospital for the injured. There were 40 or so service patients there but none of them mentally ill, so the padded cell was removed lest it encouraged Hess with his delusions. 'Arrangements were made to provide quarters for "Jonathan", secluded from other patients and given satisfactory security'. This only required a guard of 3 officers and 20 other ranks(!). The rumour is that Hess spent a night at Talgarth Military Hospital on his way to Maindiff Court on 25 June 1942, but this cannot be proved.

This, however, is not quite the end of the story. On Sunday, 11 October 1942, over three months after Hess's arrival in Wales, Dr Rast wrote in his diary:

> Hess seems to be here in Talgarth, but one is not to know it.
> He has delusions. I had samples of wine and vitamins analysed on behalf of Thurnheer.

Rast may well have known Thurnheer as they were both Swiss, and living in London. The implication is clear. Hess visited Talgarth for treatment on at least one occasion – and why not more? He was 'imprisoned' at Maindiff Court but was taken on car trips through the countryside and allowed some freedom. In fact, he was quite a well-known figure locally nicknamed 'The Kaiser of Abergavenny'.

At the War's end Hess was returned to Germany and tried at the Nuremberg International Military Tribunal, still clutching samples of food he claimed had been poisoned by the British. He also claimed during the trial that he suffered from amnesia but admitted later that this was a ruse. He was given a life sentence for 'crimes against peace' and 'conspiracy with other German leaders to commit crimes'. He was incarcerated in Spandau Prison in Berlin, where he killed himself on 17 August 1987, aged 93.

The strange case of Arnold Buchthal

Jill Fawke of the Talgarth History Society has given me another story of Camp 234, this time not of a POW but of a European refugee who, incredibly, served with the Pioneer Corps at Talgarth. It comes from a 'Life Stories' interview conducted at the British Library in 2010. The interviewee is Dame Stephanie Shirley, a pioneer of information technology in the UK, who was born in Dortmund, Germany in 1933. Her father was Arnold Buchthal, an eminent judge, who was dismissed from his post in Dortmund by the Nazis because he was a Jew. My paraphrase of the sound interview (which may be found online) continues:

> Arnold Buchthal and his family moved to Vienna and in 1939 they became refugees. The children managed to get to England on a 'Kindertransport' [a rescue effort that transported thousands of Jewish children from Germany and Austria to the UK in the nine months before the outbreak of war], while Arnold walked over the mountains from Vienna to neutral Switzerland and thence to England. Here he was interned as an enemy alien and in 1940 transported to Australia where, by coincidence, he was placed in a camp at Hay in New South Wales. He was allowed back into England to serve in the Pioneer Corps where [in 1943?] he was stationed at Bicester. Someone said he could do better than 'dig ditches', so he was sent to be a guard with the

Pioneer Corps at a mental hospital in Talgarth in South Wales. It was used as a mental hospital for German and Italian POWs.

He finished up as an administrator and changed his name to White. He was Staff Sergeant White [and likely he worked directly to Lt Colonel Drummond]. One day a group of VIPs visited and were introduced to this eminent German judge working in the camp office. 'I'm a friendly enemy alien' he said, using his official categorisation.

After the War, Staff Sergeant White left Talgarth and emigrated to the United States where he changed his name back to Buchthal and became a District Attorney. His marriage had not survived the traumas of war and exile and he divorced his wife in 1950. Coincidentally again, from a Talgarth point of view, after the war he gave evidence at the Nuremberg War Trials, though not at the same trial that saw Rudolf Hess in the dock.

The soldiers left behind

By the end of 1947 the War Department had released back to the Visiting Committee the remainder of the beds occupied by mentally ill POWs. But what was to become of their former occupants? Most were returned home in whatever condition they were in, but some had to stay. One was the poor lost soul Serefino M———-. The Visiting Committee reported in June:

Serefino M——— went to France after the Spanish Civil War where he was interned successively by French and Germans. Following the liberation of France, he came to this country as a German POW. Because of strange behaviour at his camp he was seen by a psychiatrist who recommended admission to the military hospital here. With the aid of an interpreter we diagnosed delusions and hallucinations. He believed that

Italian and German POW graves in Hay Cemetery

his wife, parents and sister were in the hospital with him and he could hear their voices addressing him. He is dull, detached and self-absorbed. He has been transferred to civilian status and admitted to this hospital because of the impending disbandment of the military hospital.

Others were at death's door, or had died since the end of the War; perhaps they were too ill to be repatriated. In Hay-on-Wye cemetery are buried 14 German and Italian POWs who died at Camp 234 between April 1945 and January 1948. They were mostly in their 30s and 40s. The graves are beautifully maintained by the Commonwealth War Graves Commission and among them is one of a British soldier from the Royal Army Ordinance Corps who also died in Talgarth. They are allies in death.

The Mid Wales Joint Counties Mental Hospital was once again a civilian hospital. The surviving patients returned with their staff from Hereford, Carmarthen and Denbigh. Yet for at least the next thirty years the violence of war haunted the male wards. Gerald McArthey, who became the Senior

Nursing Officer in 1973, told me that after the war there was 'a tremendous number of ex-soldiers in the hospital', some of them still suffering from post-traumatic stress (as shell shock was now known) and others from GPI (General Paralysis of the Insane caused by syphilis). Some were violent. Bill Devereux had experience of this when he became a nurse in the 1950s:

> There were ex-SAS and commandos in the Mid Wales [the SAS headquarters was and is near Hereford]. Some got so violent you needed 6–8 members of staff to restrain them. You needed to truss them up in straitjackets like chickens. One or two of them were war heroes. One had been a member of the Goldfish Club, meaning he had been shot down twice over the sea. Another had been in the commandos and he'd had his trigger finger cut off by the Nazis. I remember he grabbed a carving knife once and chased another patient round the ward. We had about 14 Poles here when I started [perhaps they had been members of the Free Polish Army?]. I'm not racist, mind, but I didn't trust them. They'd mutter together and you couldn't understand what they were saying. They would steal knives off the wards and sharpen them up. One was violent enough to be transferred to Broadmoor; I escorted him there.

Former nurse Judy Fawke, another granddaughter of the Head Male Nurse Albert Fawke, has the saddest of stories:

> I was in my third year of training so it must have been in 1975–6. There was a middle-aged patient we called Pete, though we knew hardly anything about him. He was totally compliant but he never spoke a single word all the years he was here. We knew he had been a prisoner of war, perhaps

89

in a camp near here or perhaps in this hospital. He was mute, which is a common condition of shell shock.

One day I was sitting in a ward dayroom with him watching the news on TV. An item came on about Russian violence in Lithuania. Suddenly, he began to sob his heart out. Then I realised he must have been Lithuanian. I was totally flabbergasted. I caught hold of his hand. He let me. What else could I do? He still didn't say anything but he sobbed and sobbed.

He died soon afterwards.

Also in the 1970s, the RAF Association Club in Talgarth used to hold a Christmas Party to which the ex-servicemen in the Mid Wales were always invited. They included a former Spitfire pilot, a gunner from a bomber, several Polish airmen; some sailors and soldiers too. They were by that time on the long-stay wards, but those who were able were escorted down to the Club by hospital staff where they received free drinks, food and cigarettes for the afternoon.

The civilian hospital 1940–1947

During the War, Medical Superintendent Peter Drummond and his staff still had 100 or so civilian mental patients under their charge and almost a full complement of over 350 again by 1947. The Letter Books for these years are kept in the Powys County Archive and I have selected a few that show how the Hospital responded to the needs of War. Most of the letters are written by Drummond.

11 January 1943
Mrs Freda D———, wife of [Army number, name and service] was a certified patient at this hospital June–September 1942 when she was discharged. Separation from her husband was the exciting cause of this patient's

breakdown and a similar occurrence would be likely to precipitate a relapse.

3 Feb 1943
Dear Mr Harper,
I am unable to grant your request to bring your wife to the pictures on Sat. evening. They are supplied by ENSA [Entertainments National Service Association] to be shown only to patients and staff and I have already gone beyond my obligations in allowing some of the staff wives to see them.

17 June 1943
To W.D. and H.O. Wills, Bristol,
My committee would be obliged if you would see your way to grant an extra allocation of cigarettes to the 315 Military Patients and 120 Military Staff at the hospital.

17 August 1944
To W.H. ——
Following your visit to your father on the 11th instant this patient was found to have a knife in his possession. I understand this knife was given to him by you in a parcel which you left with him. Since he made an attack on the Head Male Nurse one day with a knife the greatest care has been taken to see that he did not keep this weapon in his possession.
By smuggling a knife to a certified patient in a mental hospital you committed a grave offence under the law.

20 Feb 1946

To: A.W.F.———

One must feel of course a great deal of sympathy with these ex-prisoners of war [in Germany or perhaps the Far East] who find difficulty in adapting themselves after release. When he arrived here he a got a bit of a shock and he realised that he had been playing the fool. I am sure he never had any intention of committing suicide. The only behavioural disorder he showed when he came here was a degree of worry at finding himself in a mental hospital. He has been discharged.

The Mid Wales Hospital at the end of the war

The General Nursing Council sent a Committee to report on the Mid Wales in September 1947 when it was just about to revert to being a civilian hospital. From the nursing viewpoint the report was depressing:

Number of beds 330

Departments

There are the usual utility departments with a separate laundry for staff washing. There is an occupational therapy department for men but not women. There is no [operating] theatre so when operations are done the dental room is used. Leucotomies are done in this way.

Welfare of Staff

Nurses were sent away at the outbreak of war with the patients who were evacuated. Few female nurses have returned. Recruitment has almost ceased and is solely from the locality. There are no domestics on the wards and the patients are expected to do the work [one infers a good deal falls on the nurses]. Sluicing of foul linen is done by nursing staff in ward units.

Remarks

This hospital is handicapped by its isolated position and by a severe staff shortage, particularly on the female side. It is doubtful if the wards now occupied by German POWs will be able to be put to civilian use again because of staff shortage.

Staff welfare leaves a lot to be desired. There are no wardrobes in staff rooms, nurses have meals at night in the ward kitchens and nurses occupying the ward rooms need to go to the staff block for baths.

Student nurses only get 25 shillings a week and many help to support their homes. Matron says the laundry maids are a better type than the nurses and they get 11 shillings a week more than the student nurses.

With the Mid Wales Joint Counties Mental Hospital in urgent need of care and attention a new nanny was on the way. The National Health Services Act was passed on 5 July 1948 and the hospital joined the so-called Welfare State. It became part of a group of hospitals under the Welsh Border Hospital Management Committee, the others being former workhouses turned hospitals for the mentally deficient in Montgomeryshire; Brynhyfryd at Forden and Llys Maldwyn Hospital at Caersws. Both are now closed. From the patients' point of view this meant that they were no longer paid for out of the rates but from general taxation; and they could claim limited National Sickness Benefit.

Lt Colonel Drummond retired after 35 years at Talgarth, first as Assistant Medical Officer and then from 1923 as Medical Superintendent. He was succeeded by Dr Gordon Diggle, Deputy Medical Superintendent at St Matthew's Hospital, Lichfield, at a salary of £1,000 a year. At the time of his appointment he was the youngest Medical Superintendent in the country. Monty Graham, who joined as an assistant nurse in 1963, has a clear memory of him:

He was a very tall gangly man, very uncoordinated. You'd have to give him two yards because his arms and legs were all over the place. He was big, six foot two-ish, about 14 or 15 stone, highly intelligent. He was an amazing man to talk to and I recall him talking about the atom bomb and the components of it and you were looking at him and wondering what all that was about. But if you asked him about the cost of sugar I don't think he would be able to tell you.

Despite the staff shortages caused by the isolation of Talgarth there were 16 applicants.

Diggle was a man of ideas who kept up with the times; innovation now replaced tradition and a brave new world beckoned.

Chapter Three
O, Brave New World!

Young Delcie Davies applied to become Dr Diggle's secretary just when the National Health Service started in the summer of 1948:

> I walked up the drive and into the boardroom. I remember big leather seats around a U-shaped table and all the Hospital Management Committee was sitting round. The spare leather seat was for me. It was very intimidating; but I was never worried about the patients because I was used as a child to seeing them round Talgarth.

Delcie was given the job and soon she got to know some of the patients personally:

> When I arrived I found I was working in the boardroom. There was a big coal fire there and a patient called Gryff looked after it and all the other coal fires. He had been a patient since the beginning [45 years!]. He was quite a little man, tubby, and he muttered all the time. I used to be a bit frightened of him at first but he was quite harmless, you know?
>
> We had a patient from Shrewsbury who was on the farm ward. At about 9.30 in the morning these patients would walk past my window on the way up to the farm. Sid would always tap on my window when he came back after work with a little present for me. I might have a potato, some beetroot, some fruit but always a present from Sid.
>
> Now in 1950 I got married and I was away for a bit. One day Sid came to the window and because I wasn't there

he asked Dr Diggle 'Where be Annie?' That's what he called me: 'Where be Annie?' Dr Diggle said 'Oh Sid, she's got married'. Sid looked at him and said 'Oh, and be she fragrant?' In other words, was I pregnant?!

Dr Diggle, Delcie said, was a gentleman. He had been a Major in the War but unlike Lt Colonel Drummond who had the reputation for living up to his army rank by being both formal and authoritarian, Diggle was easy going and above all, she added, he was an innovator.

If so, then Dr Diggle was the right man at the right time because throughout the western world of mental hospitals a determination was growing to find 'magic bullets', new techniques of psycho-surgery to stop the endless flow of incurable schizophrenics and institutionalised depressives who were clogging up the wards of the old asylums. According to the highly respected Professor Roy Porter, writing primarily about state-run mental hospitals in the United States (in *Madness, a Brief History*), 'there must have been millions of lost and mad souls, some of them stuck in concentration-camp conditions', whose fate was settled only by death. In these depressing circumstances, Professor Porter continued, 'any attempt at cure seemed better than none. Did not the old medical adage state that desperate conditions required desperate remedies?' And so, 'medical treatment saw striking therapeutic innovations, some effective, many dubious, a few dangerous'. And so it was at the Mid Wales under Dr Diggle's leadership.

Conditions at the Mid Wales were certainly bad enough to justify experimenting with new treatments. The Welsh Border Hospital Management Report for 1953 was seriously concerned with the overcrowding of wards for the elderly, many of them senile, which was actually breaking the law. There were 500 patients, for numbers had increased dramatically since 1947, some on wards where the beds were so squashed together that they lacked lockers in between. Many patients were dangerous, particularly those on the so-called Refractory Wards. To a young nurse like Brian Devereux, the younger brother of Bill, who became an assistant nurse in 1953 when he was 17:

> There were a lot of maniacs about, particularly manic depressives. Some were completely mad. You couldn't do a bloody thing with them. We had one called P——— who was as mad as ever could be. He used to defecate on the ward, smear it all over and cover himself in horsehair that he had ripped out of the furniture. He was like a bear, you know. To get him to bath in the mornings…
>
> Others were schizophrenics who would fight their hallucinations: I mean fight them. When you tried to help you'd be attacked too. Then others would join in. As for the language shouted out – it was terrible!
>
> It was a very different place then than even 20 years later. I can remember when I first started, I'd only been there a week, this patient escaped. He climbed the gate and jumped over. I was the only one who saw him and I was a new kid, just 17. I was told to run and get him. He was running up the road and I was running behind him. I thought I've got to get him so I caught him – and luckily he started laughing.

Matron Mary Mawr had arrived in the War as a Queen Alexandra nurse after Matron Lawrence had resigned. She looked the part with her cape, badges and white muslin cap and was, by all accounts, formidable. One day she came into the boardroom where Delcie Davies was taking diction from Dr Diggle:

> Matron came in looking very dishevelled. She'd made the mistake of going up the back staircase into a female ward on her own and she'd been attacked. She'd been bitten by one

of the patients, until being rescued by the patient's twin sister. I remember Dr Diggle saying to her: 'It's your fault, you know the rules, you had no business going up there on your own'. He wasn't very sympathetic but it must have been quite an experience for her.

Dr Diggle may have added 'Crikey, I'll leave it to you,' which was his catchphrase when he would rather be somewhere else.

(The twin sisters, incidentally, had a story to tell. According to a senior nurse who later saw their case notes, one of the girls had been put away in the 1930s because she had given birth to an illegitimate baby, and her sister had accompanied her simply because she was her twin; it is possible that they were also, in the language of the times, mentally defective.)

But now help was at hand with a variety of treatments. According to the same Management Report of 1953, 'Treatments include electroconvulsive therapy (with and without muscle relaxant), electro-narcosis, modified insulin and narco-analysis, as well as occupational and recreational therapies'. The most controversial operation, frontal leucotomy, had just stopped, having been introduced to the Mid Wales in 1947.

And so, under Dr Diggle, the 'brave new world' dawned, later than elsewhere but bringing hope – and fear – over the horizon. How effective were these treatments and what was it like to administer them?

Frontal leucotomy

In April 1947 the Visiting Committee authorised the Mid Wales hospital to obtain the services of Mr Wylie McKissock to carry out prefrontal leucotomy operations 'on patients considered suitable' for a fee of 20 guineas per patient. He only came down from London once or twice a year, parking his Rolls Royce conspicuously on the drive, as Delcie Davies recalled, but this was enough to make him quite a lot of money, for McKissock was a speedy worker. He wrote in *The Lancet*:

Wylie McKissock OBE, Britain's most prolific leucotomist

This is not a time-consuming operation. A competent team in a well-organised mental hospital can do four such operations in 2–2.5 hours. The actual bilateral prefrontal leucotomy can be done by a properly trained neurosurgeon in six minutes and seldom takes more than ten minutes.

Although he said he was not gregarious he was quite a show-off, enjoying the near disbelief of watching colleagues when they saw how fast he worked. Today's NHS would have been proud of him. McKissock was the most prolific leucotomist in the country. By the late 1950s he had performed about 3,000 operations all over the South of England, the Midlands and Wales. He was also most eminent, becoming President of the Society of British Neurological Surgeons and head of the neurosurgical unit at the famous Atkinson Morley Hospital in London. So what did he do at the Mid Wales?

Working in the dental surgery – for why not drill holes in the head if drilling holes in teeth is commonplace? – McKissock would drill a hole about 1.5–2.00cm in diameter through the patient's skull on each side of the head above and behind the eyes. Through this hole, first one and then the other, he would insert either a spatula or a surgical instrument called a leucotome (from the Greek word meaning 'clear' or 'white'). This was a cannula with a retractable wire loop at the end which, when rotated, would cut the white matter of the frontal lobes – rather like cutting cheese. It was thought that psychotics had a malfunction of the cells or the grouping of the cells in the frontal lobes that resulted in obsessions, delusions and other symptoms. So the intention was to sever the connections between the frontal lobes and the deeper structures of the brain behind. This is a paraphrase of the writing of the American neurosurgeon Dr Walter Freeman and it was his technique that McKissock followed. It was a matter of faulty wiring, said Freeman, of removing the brain circuits of the frontal lobes of psychotics. It was expected that the brain would adjust to such an injury.

To be fair to Wylie McKissock, he did not expect his patients to be cured of mental illness but he did hope that after a leucotomy they would manage life better:

> The patients are made happier and can generally lead a better
> life in the institution, even if they do not recover to an extent

sufficient for them to take up a normal social position. There is a loss of function of varying degree, sometimes grave and incapacitating. No sensible surgeon would pretend that frontal leucotomy is the perfect form of treatment, but it does lead to the relief of much suffering.

Freeman put this more graphically. He used the term 'surgically induced childhood' which left the patient with an 'infantile personality'. He described one woman after a leucotomy as being 'a smiling, lazy and satisfactory patient with the personality of an oyster'. She could not remember Freeman's name and endlessly poured coffee from an empty pot. To the staff of mental hospitals overflowing with dangerous or difficult patients the benefits were clear; as in the film *One Flew Over the Cuckoo's Nest*, where the troublesome Randle McMurphy (played by Jack Nicholson) is reduced to a zombie after attacking a ward sister.

Walter Freeman gave President Kennedy's sister Rosemary a leucotomy in 1941, after which she was reduced to a speechless and incontinent two-year old.

Undeterred, Walter Freeman developed a simpler technique that did not require even the semblance of an operating theatre.

He took an ice pick from his kitchen drawer and, after experimenting on grapefruit, hammered it into a patient's brain above the eyelid and through the eye socket. Then he pivoted it so the tip severed the white matter connecting the prefrontal cortex with the brain behind. He suggested that if no anaesthetic was available then the patient could be rendered unconscious by ECT. There being no shortage of patients – and what say did they have in the matter? – he toured the mental hospitals of the United States in his van called his 'lobotomobile', and charged $25 per operation. He gave interviews while he was operating and on one occasion lost his concentration so that the ice pick slipped and the patient died. By 1951 nearly 20,000 mental patients had been leucotomised (or lobotomised) in the USA.

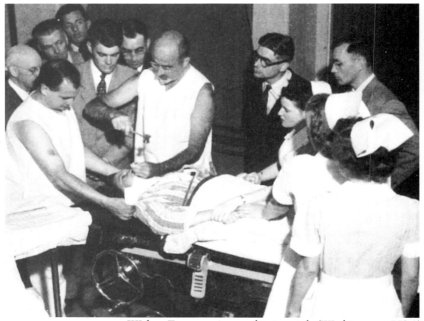

Walter Freeman inserts his ice pick (Washington, USA)

The controversy that had always surrounded leucotomy – how do you balance benefit with risk? – now combined with distaste at the flamboyance of Freeman to cause a backlash. Leucotomies went out of fashion in the United States and then the new generation of anti-psychotic drugs removed the need. Wylie McKissock went on to invent a new technique called Rostral Leucotomy which was a much scaled down version of its predecessor. It was intended to achieve the same degree of recovery for a smaller cost and was recommended not for psychotics but for psycho-neurotics. Here a needle was inserted into the brain and much more limited excavation carried on inside. McKissock did not work at the Mid Wales after 1952. Revealingly, his long obituary in the *Independent* newspaper did not mention his leucotomy work at all.

When Doctor Hession arrived in 1977 there were still several leucotomised patients on the wards, almost 30 years after their operations.

The last word here is from a British psychiatrist who, in 1950, followed up 300 patients who had been leucotomised. He said that the operation 'reduced the complexity of psychic life'. For most of them, activity was replaced by inertia; they were left emotionally blunted and intellectually restricted. A few were severely brain damaged and a few left hospital for responsible work. Five per cent died during the operation.

Electroconvulsive therapy (ECT)

In the history of treating insanity there used to be the persistent belief that severe physical and psychological shock could result in recovery. Terror was used as a therapy for lunatics since antiquity: half drowning, for example, or in eighteenth-century British institutions rotatory machines into which the lunatic was strapped resulting in 'instant discharge of the content of the bowels, bladder and stomach'. Presumably, if all else failed then terror of the treatment would subconsciously suppress the behaviour of the mad.

Cardiazol injections were given to both POWs and civilian patients in the Talgarth Military Hospital during the war with the intention of causing convulsions, like an epileptic fit, which were intended to reduce severe depression. Elsewhere, there is evidence that this treatment had an element of purposeful terror: 'we heard our patients objecting violently to the anticipated attack and vainly exerting all their willpower to fight it off' was a description used in another hospital. There were elements of cruelty and voyeurism too. The staff of the Psychiatric Institute at the University of Illinois studied the effects of Metrazol injections (another name for Cardiazol) by watching film of male and female patients who were made to strip naked in a group and then convulsed.

ECT was introduced into the UK because it was cheaper and easier to administer than Cardiazol.

At Talgarth, the first 'Electro-Convulsant Apparatus similar to the one recently obtained for the Military Unit' was ordered by Medical Superintendent Drummond in August 1942 for the cost of £60. Patients who had been 'detained', or certified, by the Lunacy Act of 1890 had no right to reject any form of treatment, and that included ECT. This remained true under the Mental Health Act of 1959 (see later) which gave psychiatrists authority to treat certified ('sectioned') patients without consent. For example, in July 1944 Peter Drummond wrote to the relatives of Mrs H——- who was a voluntary patient:

> She has refused to receive electrical treatment and I was quite unable to persuade her to remain in hospital. She has become very agitated and worried. If she becomes troublesome at home, then consideration should be given to admitting her as a certified patient.

The definition of ECT, sometimes known as electroshock therapy, is 'a psychiatric treatment in which seizures are electrically induced in patients to provide relief from mental disorder'. An electric current is passed through the patient's brain via electric terminals connected either side of the patient's head. This triggers a split second shock that induces instant convulsion.

It seemed to the pioneers of ECT that the shock was the jolt necessary to free the mind from deep depression. Another early explanation of the effect of ECT was that 'it knocked out, transiently or permanently, diseased nerve cells which are less resistant than healthy cells', in the same way that radiotherapy is now used in cancer treatment. That reasoning is no longer used, and experts are not clear what exactly causes the electro-chemical effect in the brain that can cure depression. But the consensus is that it works for sufferers from severe depression. The definition quoted above continues 'a round of ECT is effective for about 50 per cent of people with treatment resistant major depressive disorder... but about half the patients relapse within twelve months' (Wikipedia on ECT, footnotes 6 and 7).

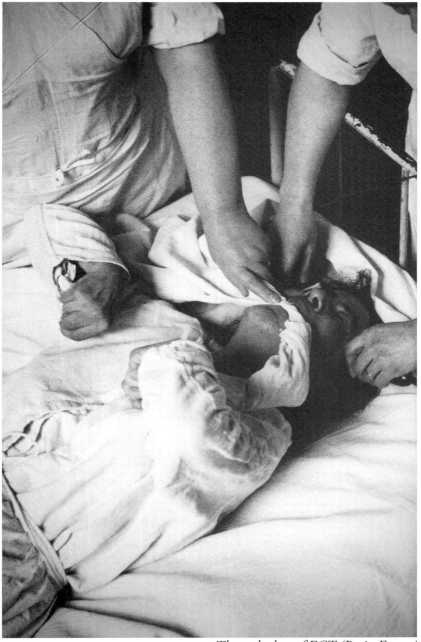

The early days of ECT (Paris, France)

There were recognised dangers from the start. ECT on its own could cause convulsions so violent that bones were broken, even the spine. So doctors began to experiment by preceding ECT with an injection of curare, the muscle-paralysing South American poison, in order to modify the convulsion. In 1951 this was replaced by succinylcholine which was a safer, synthetic, alternative. However, this muscle paralyser had the terrifying effect on the patient, in those seconds before ECT was applied, of feeling suffocated and unable to move; so a short-acting anaesthetic was given as well. By the end of the 1950s most mental hospitals used this form of modified ECT.

There were/are other dangers too. ECT frequently caused confusion and short-term memory loss, as do other anaesthetics. More serious was overuse. It was found that giving ECT many times a day for many days could reduce patients to the status of a 'vegetable' so that they became incontinent and required artificial feeding. This was known as 'regressive ECT'.

All these experiences of ECT in the early days were replicated at the Mid Wales. One of the nurses who helped to administer it was Bill Devereux:

> The best thing that worked in the 1950s and 60s as opposed to today for certain patients was ECT, electro-convulsive therapy. And it worked well for depressives. Now when they started that because of the contractions, having the fit, you could break bones. So you had four nurses to a patient, holding him, so he didn't snap any bones. Then they decided they'd give them curare which is the old fashioned thing Amazon Indians put on their arrows which paralysed the enemy. But if I gave you curare just prior to giving ECT what a frightening thing you'd have because you wouldn't be able to move a muscle! It would frighten the hell out of you, wouldn't it? So when they found that out Pentothal was used to put you to sleep…

Pentothal is the equivalent to succinylcholine and was used in USA death cells before the lethal injection.

Joan, who later married Bill's brother, Brian Devereux, was a student nurse working on the wards in the late 1950s:

> My first memory of ECT as a student: there wasn't a proper treatment room so I was sent to clear part of one dormitory and prepare the space. We weren't really given any idea of what was going to happen and on that first occasion I found it terrifying because the ECT was given straight. I found the whole thing quite scary. As an observer I stood at the end of the bed and I had this full-on view of the convulsion.
>
> Us nurses had to make the gags, mouth gags to give the patient something to bite on. We used two spatulas because one would split and we wrapped them in lint and hand stitched them together.
>
> Then the anaesthetic came in and then they built a designated treatment centre which led off a corridor by Female Ward 7. This had an ECT room, the dentists and physiotherapy.

> *Brian:* The first time I saw ECT done was in the second dormitory on Male 1. There was a box with electrodes leading to the patient's head. Then the doctor pressed the button and as soon as the patient went into convulsion you pushed your hands under him to support his back because there were dangers of breaking his spine. There was a terrific convulsion. Then the Pentothal was used and you didn't see the half of it.
>
> ECT did a lot of good. Some of the women patients were very, very depressed, wouldn't even speak, some of

them. Then after one or two treatments they were as right as rain. It might not last but for a short while it worked. There was one male patient, T——, who insisted on it; said it was the only way to stop his depressions. He had hundreds of ECT sessions, but he became quite stupefied towards the end of his life.

It was also given to really bad schizophrenics who were really mad and it sort of brought them round but I don't think it really worked.

Gerald McArthey, who was the Senior Nursing Officer at the Mid Wales in the 1970s, was more sceptical:

Well, if you cut your leg and you apply some sort of medication and then a dressing you know you are doing something for the leg, right? ECT just exploded in the brain. There was no guarantee. I mean, you could have a session or six sessions, whatever, and you never knew. Some patients had ECT on and off for years.

That was the trouble at the Mid Wales. There were no patient records available to nurses and ECT seems to have been given as a matter of routine. Some nurses from this era say that ECT was used sparingly but Dr Diggle told the Welsh Border Hospital Management Committee in 1961 that, according to the last annual return, 'the hospital had given 2500 treatments of ECT', that's an average of 50 treatments every week. Gerald McCarthy implied that ECT had been used as a deterrent; 'You had straight ECT for violent people, mostly schizophrenics, and modified ECT with an anaesthetic for the others, which was more acceptable'. If ECT was given as a punishment or deterrent at Talgarth then that was no different from elsewhere. A report in *The Lancet* as late as 1986 described the administration of ECT as 'deeply disturbing'. Attendant staff were 'generally hostile to ECT and viewed the procedure as controlling and, punishing the patients'.

However, to bring the story of ECT at the Mid Wales up to date, from the 1970s it was administered a few times a week in the Treatment Centre. According to one or two nurses involved, an anaesthetist would inject the patient into sleep, a doctor would apply the ECT with another doctor present. A nurse would hold the patient's hand – 'that's not really restraint' – and a gag would protect the mouth during convulsions. Dr Michael Hession, a Senior Consultant from 1977, has no doubt that ECT had its uses – and abuses:

> It's a miracle drug in the treatment of certain types of very severe intractable depression which don't respond to anti-depressants, and to certain types of obsessive-compulsive disorders which don't respond to medication. You can see a most dramatic response.

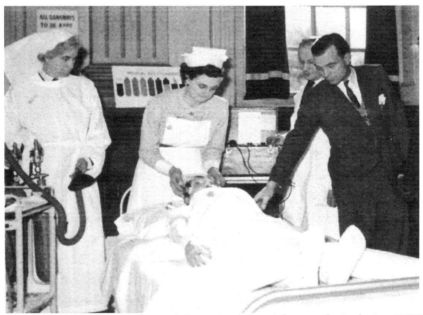

Matron Mawr stands by with anaesthetic during ECT

But the general recommendations now are that the patient should have failed to respond to three different anti-psychotic or anti-depressant medications before ECT is used and the dose is carefully monitored.

As a postscript to the use of ECT at Talgarth, former nurse David Lewis told me that when he arrived as a young nurse in the 1960s he would find two rotas put up daily for the likes of him: four strong males on standby to help with ECT, and four strong males on standby as pallbearers to carry the coffins of deceased patients from the makeshift mortuary to the burial site.

Deep sleep treatments

Explorers into the brave new world of psychosurgery reported excitedly about their findings. Initially these findings were given medical approval only to be exposed later as false, with the partial exception of ECT. The need to arrest somehow the hopeless increase in incurable and institutionalised mental patients accounts for this optimism and desperation too. Nowhere is this truer than in the application of deep sleep therapy at the Mid Wales Mental Hospital in the 1950s and 60s.

The General Nursing Council Report on the Mid Wales in 1953 said 'Treatments include ECT (with or without muscle relaxant) electro-narcosis and modified insulin'. These days, electro-narcosis or the rendering of unconsciousness after electric shock is used as the first stage in animal slaughter. In the treatment of the mentally ill at this time it was a technique to induce prolonged sleep by repeated, low amplitude, electric current passing though the brain. In other words, it was a spin-off from ECT, which was sometimes used as an anaesthetic in itself. It was said to be beneficial for patients with anxiety, depression and schizophrenia. An alternative treatment was the repeated injection of large doses of insulin under medical supervision. This induced coma, lasting for many hours would be brought to an end by giving glucose, either through the nose or intravenously. David Lewis told me that at the Mid Wales 'Insulin injections were used in the 1950s. They induced an eighteen-hour coma after which the patient was brought round with sugar'.

An advantage of deep sleep therapy was that the patient had no knowledge of it afterwards. The famous singer Toni Lamond described her experience in an Australian hospital in her autobiography *First Half*:

> I was given a semi-private room. On the way to it I saw several beds along the corridors with sleeping patients. The patient in the other bed in my room was also asleep. I thought nothing of it at the time. Although it was mid-morning, the stillness was eerie for a hospital that looked to be full to overflowing. I was given a handful of pills to take and the next thing I remember was Dr Bailey standing by the bed asking how I felt. I told him I'd had a good night's sleep. He laughed and informed me it was ten days later and, what's more, he had taken some weight off me. I was checked out of the hospital and this time noticed the other patients were still asleep or being taken to the bathroom while out on their feet.

The disadvantage, from the patient's point of view, was that they could be given all kinds of treatment while deeply asleep that they were not aware of: ECT, drugs, or in the ominous words of one textbook 'physical treatment necessary but often not tolerated'. Perhaps that is why a scandal at Toni Lamond's hospital in the 1960s found that 26 patients had died as a result of the insulin coma. The medical justification for insulin at this time was that 'it counteracts the schizophrenic process' and the common sense, though fallacious, justification for DICT (Deep Insulin Coma Therapy) was that a long sleep would quieten and refresh the troubled mind. In fact, medical opinion turned against DICT, beginning with an influential *Lancet* article in November 1953 by Harold Bourne, 'The Insulin Myth', and culminating in another in 1957 by Brian Ackner of the Bethlem Hospital that concluded insulin 'was not a specific therapeutic agent'. It was a clutching at straws, another supposed psycho-surgery breakthrough that was about to be superceded by the chemical revolution. It was not used at the Mid Wales after the 1950s.

The chemical revolution

In the late 1950s a drug arrived at the Mid Wales that was claimed to combat mental illness almost as effectively as penicillin killed bacterial infection. It's trade name was Largactil, known as the 'liquid cosh', and it was manufactured from chlorpromazine, the anti-psychotic and anti-depressant compound. Dr Hession remembered:

> The people in Talgarth down the bottom of the hill used to hear the noise of the hospital. There was banging and shouting – people banging the radiators – just out of sheer boredom and frustration, as well as the general noise of a mental hospital [Several former nurses refute that the sounds could possibly have travelled so far]. And then Largactil or chlorpromazine came in. Largactil was the first anti-psychotic drug and people down in the village said that within three months the hospital had gone quiet. Disturbed people had all been treated with this new wonder drug and it had calmed them down. There were complications, of course, like jaundice, from the big doses that were used.

Joan Devereux remembers the first time she administered it:

> Largactil didn't come in until we'd been here for a few years but I'll never forget the first time I gave it to a patient. The lady turned yellow, oh gosh! She was jaundiced because of

the drug. Well, I think the dosage was a bit hit and miss when we were trialling these drugs.

The influential British psychiatrist William Sargant went so far as to claim that drugs like Largactil and the powerful anti-depressant Imipramine would eliminate mental illness by the twenty-first century, which shows how desperate psychiatrists were to get out of the old asylum mentality. Certainly, in this brave new world it was the drugs that reached the new horizon while the surgery was cast into darkness. Largactil worked though it caused severe drowsiness and dizziness. At the Mid Wales nurse Gladys Davies, who started in 1949 and left 20 years later, wrote towards the end of her time:

> Our work is made much easier because of modern drugs. I had one patient who hardly spoke half-a-dozen sentences during a year. She would crouch under the table like a dog, or go and kick the door like a pony. But the new drug given to her by injection and followed up by tablets of the same drug [surely Largactil, which was administered in this way] made a miraculous new person of her. Before her breakdown of about 12 years' duration, she had been a therapy teacher; it was wonderful to see her come round and able to do beautiful needlework again, eat her food again, hold a conversation and help with the routine of the ward. She was put on parole and in due course discharged – she was rather an exceptional case.

Another anti-psychotic drug administered in the early days was Sparine. But it is paraldehyde that is remembered by many nurses from the 50s and 60s because of its unpleasant side effects. Its original use had been as a suppressant of epilepsy but it became irresistible, to many, as another sedative. It was a liquid that made the breath smell foul because so much of it was excreted through the lungs. Bill Devereux used it for its original purpose:

> Oh, paraldehyde! It was a liquid that looked like turps [turpentine] but it wasn't mixed with water. It came in little bottles which you had to shake up until it was all little bubbles floating in suspension. It was an excellent drug for *status epilepticus* – a status was when a patient went into one epileptic fit after another, after another. You gave an injection of paraldehyde and that stopped it.

Joan and Brian Devereux remember it as an addictive sedative, taken by mouth:

> *Brian:* They had it in bottles and you'd see the paraldehyde, like, solid on top and you had to shake it down and they drank it. Some of them were quite addicted because they guzzled it down.
>
> *Joan:* Oh yeah, we had two patients in particular in Female 3 [ward] who were no doubt addicted because they would howl and scream until they got their dose, as they called it.
>
> *Brian:* And when it had worn off they'd be going at it again. There was no treatment about it. It just calmed you down. It didn't make you better.

Psycho-pharmacology gave a huge boost to psychiatrists and huge profits to the pharmaceutical industry. From the 1970s and 80s drugs like Valium as a tranquillizer and Prozac as an anti-depressant became the most prescribed medicines for the general public. For the mentally ill – and the very existence of these drugs broke down a barrier between 'sane' and 'insane' – the heavier drugs beginning with Largactil meant that more patients could be treated as outpatients. It also meant that risky surgery and therapy could be avoided. Moreover, drugs were cost effective (then) and this pleased the politicians. At the Mid Wales, as in all other mental hospitals, change was on the way.

Keith Parry joined the Mid Wales as a trainee nurse in 1961 and ended his career there as the last Manager, leaving when the Hospital closed in 2000. He witnessed at first hand the violence on some wards before drugs, the effect of drugs and, later, the beneficial effects of outdoor therapy. His arrival, incidentally, was typical of the many staff who joined straight from school in Talgarth and spent their careers 'up top':

> I was living in Talgarth and I was in the Square one Saturday morning at the start of the summer holidays when my father got talking to the Chief Male Nurse. He turned to me and said 'Why don't you come "up top" and get some holiday money?' So that's how I started as a teenage Nursing Assistant.

His first day was truly frightening:

> I went to the Office where one of the chief male nurses was sat. He gave me some white coats and my keys and he said 'You're working on Male 3, Keith' [the Refractory Ward with violent patients]. So there I am, just 18, and I unlocked the door to go into this ward and – as true as I'm sat here now – I was walking down the corridor into the day room when a guy, a 20-stone guy, came at me down the corridor with a chair above his head shouting: 'They've got to be shot! They've got to be shot!' That's true! In fact, he was a gentle giant and that was just one of his sayings but I thought he was going for me!

Keith Parry did have to fight off two violent patients over the next year or so. One 'very psychotic, very bizarre guy' attacked him when they were virtually alone on the ward as most of the patients and nurses were at the film screening one Friday evening. Another time, one night when he was sitting on the end of a bed talking to a former farmer, the patient suddenly hallucinated that Keith was a sheep-stealer: 'he went for me and we were rolling around on the floor until the night medical officer did his round. He was very disturbed, poor guy, and he didn't even remember the incident, thankfully so'.

Keith Parry went on to say that these incidents were in the very early days of anti-psychotic drugs and they were having an effect: 'before the era of drugs I hate to think what some of the wards were like'. However, he continued, while no doubt some of the violence on the difficult wards was due to schizophrenia, or manic depression or psychopathic behaviour in ex-soldiers, some of it was also the effect of institutionalisation, of being cooped up year after year on a ward with nothing to do:

> At this time there were 45 beds in some wards, so one large dormitory really, and a large day room with a snooker table in the middle, so not much room to move. By day the majority of these guys would be wandering around exhibiting bizarre behaviour and getting boisterous. So it's not surprising in these early days that not many weeks went by without someone having to be restrained by putting him in a side room and turning the key.

Years later, when Keith Parry was Manager of the hospital, he made an important rediscovery:

> There was a Charge Nurse by the name of Arnold Weale, who worked on one of the more difficult male wards, one

where there was a lot of aggressive behaviour and extremely difficult people to manage. Arnold got them out into Occupational Therapy and then he decided to take it further. He called them his Project Team and he took them out apple picking, potato picking and then clearing 10 acres between small fir trees.

He got these difficult young men using hatchets and sharp blades to cut the rubbish away and there was never any trouble.

I wrote an article published in the *Nursing Times* about this because we discovered that the aggression actually reduced and medication was reduced in any activity associated with agriculture and horticulture: the patients became less aggressive and managed more independently.

So the founding fathers were right in their belief that fresh air and working on the land aids recovery. If Wern Fawr farm had not been closed down in the 1950s (see later) perhaps some of the pent-up aggression at the Mid Wales could have been avoided. But the real lesson of Keith Parry's rediscovery goes further back:

> You know, there was no history of these young men having aggressive behaviour to our knowledge prior to them being inpatients. They had learned their behaviour from others and they also learned that once patients were admitted to that place there were not many who actually left.

There is an amusing end to this story:

> One day I went up there [to the plantation] and one of the patients approached me: 'Mr Parry, Mr Parry, we don't get any breakfast these days. G— P— don't give us any

breakfast'. He was the patient who acted as cook at Tegfan [then a house in the grounds where the team lived]. So I went and spoke to him: 'G——, I understand the boys don't get breakfast anymore?'

'No', he said, 'we're too busy here in the mornings so I give it to them the night before'. That's true! He used to cook the bacon and eggs the night before.

Life on the wards

Based on the Reports of the Welsh Border Hospital Management Committee and the General Nursing Council, and also on the memories of the Devereux brothers who with their wives Sylvia and Joan all started work as nurses in the 1950s, here is a description of day-to-day life on the wards during this period.

Life centred on the wards. The sexes were segregated and of the 350-plus patients in this decade there were always fewer males than females. There were different wards for different categories of patient. For instance, in 1961 the male wards were for Admission patients (41, of whom 15 were in bed, managed by 4 staff on duty), Disturbed or Refractory patients (32 managed by 3 staff), Long-stay and Infirm (46, of whom 24 were in bed, managed by 3 staff) and Long-stay patients, 3 wards of 29, 20 and 20 elderly men, each ward managed by just 1 member of staff. The ward was home but still, a locked home.

Conditions in the day rooms improved through the 1950s so that they ended the decade being described as 'homely'. At first wirelesses and fireplaces were installed; by the end of the decade TVs and central heating. Rayburn cookers were put into the small ward kitchens and the padded cells became storerooms. Hot water found its way into the washbasins and baths. In 1961 the hospital was being rewired; there was still no electricity in the small ward kitchens and therefore no fridges nor electric sterilisers. The dormitories came in for criticism, except for the 'New Hospital' (later Wards 7 and 8) which was described as 'pleasant with good facilities for the newly admitted'. In 1961 'many dormitories are still to be modernised. They are overcrowded with poor lighting and [perhaps for this reason] have no curtains. The furnishings are shabby. There is dust everywhere'. Throughout the decade the Visiting Committees were squeamish about the cleaning facilities next to the wards: 'the sanitary annexes are in a bad state and those on the male side malodorous'.

Patients were always reported to be 'contented' and the food was always reported to be 'good'. It came in containers wheeled on trolleys down the corridors from the main kitchen, and was served by the nurse on duty (who was often still called an 'orderly' or 'attendant') and carried upstairs to those who ate in bed in the upper dormitory. The cutlery was counted in and out by the nurse, helped by a patient. There were four 'meals' a day, even if 'supper' was bread and cheese and 'afternoon tea' was tea and biscuits.

The Hospital Secretary, Gwyn Lewis (father of nurse David Lewis), was defensive about the bread and cheese:

> It is worth observing that in the country as a whole mental hospitals are allowed 14–15 shillings per week per patient while in general hospitals it is 25–50 shillings per week. Nevertheless, 4 meals a day are provided and diet is well-balanced. The main meal is dinner in the middle of the day and may consist of boiled ham, potatoes and greens with rice pudding to follow, or roast mutton with cabbage and potatoes with apricot tart and custard, or roast beef, cauliflower and mash followed by stewed rhubarb.

On the psycho-geriatric wards with considerable numbers of mentally defective patients there were those who could not feed themselves. Their menu was different. Joan Devereux recalls:

They had to be spoon fed. They used to have like a 'sop' they called it. 'Sap' Matron Mawr called it, but she was Scottish. 'Sop' because it was a bowl of bread with tea, ordinary bread dipped in, with some sugar added. And that would be their staple diet really; mint with mashed potatoes, perhaps, for dinner.

Sometimes supplies were augmented by visiting friends and family. Bill Devereux:

> Even visitors regarded the ward as home. It would be nothing for a visitor to ring me from Yorkshire and say 'Hello, Bill, will it be OK if I come and visit so-and-so today?' Then he'd come and say 'Now, Bill, I brought you some bottles today for the patients at Christmas'. In them days I can remember the visitors fetching presents for every patient on the ward and a Christmas cake for staff. All that has gone: you wouldn't be allowed to accept a present now.

On Mondays the Head Gardener (Harry Evans) would meet with the Head Chef and discuss menus. Patients from the Farm Ward, known as Tegfan, would pick vegetables and carry them into female ward rooms in large baskets where they would be prepared, as far as possible, for the kitchen – no sharp instruments allowed.

Life was not without cheer. The hospital baker, Ernie Leighton, doubled up as the bookie. Either he came up to the ward with his own key to collect bets on the horses or the ward sent a representative down to the bakery to place bets. Wandering the hospital corridors was not allowed, so the rep. would carry a loaf of bread back to the ward under his arm disguising the betting slips: 'Just been down for a loaf', he would say if accosted.

Coronation dinner in Recreation Hall, 1953. Dr Diggle and his wife in the centre turn to the camera: his Deputy Dr Hand and his wife on the left.

Cigarettes were a valued currency. Everyone seemed to smoke like chimneys, more than one nurse remembered. Patients out in Talgarth would scavenge the contents of ash trays in pubs and make roll-your-own fags. The Mid Wales had its tobacco barons, just like prisons. Newspapers were delivered to the main office and brought to the wards by the nurses. In the main Hall were three snooker tables and there was a large library.

Patients wore their own clothes, augmented by cast-off stock on each ward, which the tailor and his assistants had made good. The nurses' uniforms had changed, incidentally. Male nurses wore a white jacket with epaulettes on the shoulders to denote rank and female nurses wore a pale blue dress with a starched white apron over it. In those days, male nurses were given a three-piece serge suit when they joined to wear beneath their uniform.

In the 1950s and 60s there were very few cleaners or porters at the Mid Wales. Most of the work was done by the nurses, particularly the juniors, even though it was outside a nurse's job description. They cleaned 'fouled-linen' in the sluices off the wards – 'Oh my God', Joan said, 'you

121

Matron Mawr with her nurses, 1960

didn't like being on sluice room duty! You had to hose off the sheets and then use a scrubbing brush' – and polished the floors using the ubiquitous 'bumper' and tins of wax. Nurses carried around the food containers, and nurses were 'locked in the backs' meaning the lines of 6 semi-open lavatories and 6 wash basins attached to each ward helping 15 to 20 patients every morning and evening. Up until the 1950s there were male and female 'general bathrooms' elsewhere in the grounds where patients in one ward at a time, once a week, would take a supervised bath. It had been 'like dipping sheep' an old timer nurse told Keith Parry. But by this time the baths were in the ward units. Worst off was the junior nurse known as 'the last', who was the general dogsbody. In 1947 the *Brecon and Radnor Gazette* advertised for student nurses with a starting salary of only £75 per year. Little wonder there was a shortage of nurses.

The hospital nursing staff was hierarchical, headed up on the female side by the regal, awesome Matron Mawr.

Joan Devereux:

She would come into the ward and whatever you were doing you had to stop. You would stand and you would not speak until you were spoken to. If she went past and didn't say 'Good Morning' you didn't open your mouth.

It was the same with the doctors. You stood when they came into the ward. The only excuse was if you were giving a patient an enema behind a screen. 'Good morning, nurse', the doctor would say. You stood to attention and answered 'Good morning Sir', with the emphasis on *Sir*.

There was always that element of risk too, whether it was being left alone at night on a locked ward or handling a difficult patient. Sylvia Devereux had to cope with one who behaved like a wild animal, presumably before Largactil was available:

> I used to be terrified of one patient, just this one. She was very, very, rough, almost subnormal. She had a side room with specially reinforced doors because she used to kick and bang her head, and the door would be shaking. She was trying to get out and get at you. She said that God was under her mattress and I couldn't touch it, but I had to take it out for cleaning. How could I put it back? I was the only nurse on the ward so I got my friend Jean and said 'you put the mattress back and I'll stand here with the sheet and throw it over her if anything happens'. It was OK but God it was terrifying. I was scared stiff. I had to get staff from other wards when I gave her injections.

Incidentally, although a communal dining room for the use of male and female staff was built in 1956 – until then the sexes had eaten separately – it was not until the 1970s that male nurses worked on female wards and vice versa.

During the day patients who were suitable went to occupational therapy. In 1953 the female general bathroom was converted into a Female Occupational Therapy Department and a hairdressing salon was installed for those female patients who, said a Visiting Committee Report, 'still care about their appearance'. Two years later a Male Occupational Therapy Department followed and two occupational therapists were employed. The GNC Inspector reported in 1961:

> On the female side occupational therapy is limited. On the day of my visit 13 patients were occupied with embroidery and knitting. A further 20 were doing same on the wards and another 20 were making dishcloths. The care of the disturbed and long-stay patients in the wards would be facilitated if more active programmes were instituted. The new Male Occupational Therapy Unit is a good one having accommodation for 40. Industrial work in the form of dismantling PO telephones and bell sets is undertaken by patients who work a 30-hour week and are paid a weekly sum of money. Other patients make handicrafts which encourages contact with the village.

True to the aspiration of the founding fathers, fresh air was considered therapeutic in itself. There were gardening gangs out most days under supervision, trimming, digging, planting and harvesting on the Mid Wales farm, Wern Fawr; also for local farmers. They would come back with vegetables hidden under their overcoats and sometimes with a whiff of cider on their breath. No-one seemed to mind. Bill Devereux remembers one patient in particular:

> He was a nice, young lad, an obsessive, compulsive neurotic. In those days I added a greenhouse to my veranda and used to grow all kinds of plants. He asked me to give him lessons

and because of his illness, maybe, he couldn't leave the growing alone. He read it all up and experimented in my greenhouse. Years later I got to know someone who worked in Cardiff Parks. One time he said to me, 'So-and-so wants to be remembered to you'. He was this former patient – and now he was the boss of Cardiff Parks.

The reports speak well of the atmosphere in the Mid Wales and the gradual humanising of life there. There were two consistent complaints for which no one was to blame. The first was the remoteness of Talgarth, which meant that outside staff were hard to obtain and patients too easily forgotten by their families. The second was the problem endemic to mental hospitals: the unstoppable increase in numbers of the bedridden elderly. The Hospital Management Committee Report of 1961 concluded:

> There seemed a large number of geriatric patients who should be outside a mental hospital but Dr Diggle thought that most of the psychiatric/geriatric cases he had, had been there so long that it would be cruel and inhuman to send them into a new environment. It accounted for most of the 35 per cent of patients who were not up and about.

All the retired nurses living around Talgarth have memories of particular patients. Gladys Davies wrote down her memories covering the years after she joined in 1949. She had the knack (she died some years ago) of recalling catchphrases that bring her characters to life:

> One patient, Gwyneth, on good days would sit quietly making a rug, but after ten minutes she would turn it completely over and continue on the other side. Most days she would remind the staff that she was waiting for her coffin and if it should come, to be sure to leave her woolly hat on

and to put a hot water bottle in the coffin because she would be very cold.

Another patient, we called her Ma Murray, was a big, buxom woman who had probably been on the stage when she was younger. She would come down (she slept upstairs) and would sail in and say in a loud voice: 'Come on ladies, Monday morning – pay your rent'… and it was Monday morning.

Then there was a patient – now a frail, little old woman of about 80 – who was still quite active. One of the staff could remember her in the old days coming from Boughrood on a pony to Talgarth market with a basket on her arm, and probably in it butter, eggs and chicken to sell. In the hospital, she would say the same thing to everyone, 'You must send me down to the [Visiting] Committee to get my discharge and help me get home!'

Outpatients

During this time, outpatient clinics began to be held weekly in Brecon, Newtown and Llandrindod Wells. This no doubt facilitated treatment but it meant that the two psychiatrists at the Mid Wales, Dr Diggle and his deputy Dr Hand, together with the general medical practitioner, Dr Anderson, were frequently away for the day; three doctors to look after 350–500 patients was thin staffing at the best of times. The 1961 Inspectors Report of the GNC said: 'The work of the medical staff in such a scattered area is added to by the distance that has to be travelled to outpatient clinics and domiciliary visits'. At Whitchurch Mental Hospital in Cardiff, which was admittedly nearly twice as large as the Mid Wales, there was a unit of ten psychiatrists and other specialised staff. Dr Diggle told one visiting committee that he held very few case conferences because he could not convene enough medical staff; the nurses, incidentally, were not included.

Dr Diggle's outpatient case notes for 1948 are available in the Powys Archive. They are revealing. In the first place they show that the Mid Wales could still be a last resort for patients who were not necessarily mentally ill but had nowhere else to go:

> The patient is a widower whose son lives with him. The house was practically derelict. It was in a filthy condition. The patient was filthy. According to his son he had not changed his underclothing for nine months. He states that he sees his wife at nights, although whether this is a true hallucination is doubtful as he has always been a Spiritualist. He is harmless but conditions have gone from bad to worse.
>
> In my opinion B—— is certifiable and I think a Summary Reception Order could be used on the grounds of neglect. Which hospital he goes to depends on family financial circumstances.

In 1948 the old Lunacy Act of 1890 still applied (see above) governing 'reception orders' for admission to an asylum. The Mental Health Act of 1959 would change this by spelling out a much tighter legal framework under Sections One, Two and Three for the detention of patients in mental hospitals against their will (see below).

The 'obsessional state' (Diggle's diagnosis) of Mrs N—- who lived in Montgomeryshire must have been induced by her isolation and poverty as much as her state of mind.

> She has a continuous worry lest her breathing should stop so she has had insomnia for seven months.
>
> She is an only child. She married her second cousin who is many years older and has had four children in quick succession. She did not want to get married. The house is very isolated. She has to fetch her water some distance and

her husband will not help her. During her last pregnancy the nurse frightened her by saying she was going to have a PPH [postpartum haemorrhage]. All her symptoms date from this worry.

Dr Diggle's prescription: 'Her obsession is probably the lesser of two evils. Inpatient treatment would be of no avail. All I can recommend is a strong sedative at night – and reassurance.'

The psychiatric social worker was now D. Hodges, who also made home visits. She applied doses of common sense to everyday anxieties about mental illness:

Mrs K is a pale pretty woman who looks tired and depressed. She has two children and her husband was at home as it was his half day. She has always been nervous and highly strung with occasional fits of depression, which up until now she had shaken off. Six weeks ago she woke up suddenly feeling very frightened, shaking all over, although she had not been dreaming. She had a repeat attack and has begun to get headaches and shoulder pains. She has been told there is no physical cause and she is frightened she may be going insane. She does nothing but brood.

Prescription: 'I asked her if she had thought about part-time work. I suggested she should go to the Labour Exchange and also try on her own among the shops and cafes in the town as she would like to work among plenty of people. She said she would do this'.

The winds of change

In 1947 a small training school was established at the Mid Wales Hospital in order to attract more nurses, though Medical Superintendent Drummond was pessimistic about it. He said training would only encourage nurses to move away. It began in the Boardroom where Matron Mawr collected together 'a skeleton, disarticulate bones, a few charts and models'. So training began, under an unqualified tutor, for six student nurses and 12 temporary nurses. Soon the training school moved to the former Isolation Ward where a few patients carrying typhoid had once been segregated. Although it was registered by the General Nursing Council, its first years were a struggle. Numbers went down to four and then, in the three years 1957–1959, a modest total of 27 student nurses were recruited, of whom 14 gave up. Nearly all the students came from the locality, including the Devereux brothers and their future wives.

What was on offer was a three-year study course of 44 hours a week for 156 weeks; the rest of the time was spent nursing on the wards with practical experience gained also at hospitals in Hereford and Abergavenny. The academic training followed the SRN qualification (State Registered Nurse) with lessons, for example, in anatomy, physiology and hygiene before offering specialised classes in mental health. An advertisement in the *Montgomery Express* of September 1960 said: 'This is a recognised Training School for mental nurses under the GNC. Lectures are given by the Consultant Staff and include all modern methods of Psychiatric treatment'. It was known officially as the Powys School of Nursing and conferred on a student nurse the qualification of an RMN – Registered Mental Nurse. A shorter course qualified a pupil nurse as State Enrolled (SEN).

In 1956, to the consternation of all including the Management Committee, the Ministry of Health closed down Wern Fawr farm, as it did all other farms attached to the old asylums. Farming as an occupational therapy ceased and the following year 152 acres of farm land went under the hammer for £13,950 with a further 27 acres transferred to the Forestry

Commission. Only the eight acres of market garden remained. Even today, former nurses like Bill Devereux (whose father was the Head Storekeeper) sound outraged:

> At least 12 patients worked on the farm – I was Charge there at the time – and many of them were used to that kind of work. And then the hospital farm supplied all the eggs and vegetables and a lot of the meat which my father used to butcher. He worked out that it was cheaper to bake a loaf at a halfpenny a time than buy it in.
>
> Why did they do it? Because the do-gooders thought this kind of work was exploiting patients. Slave labour! So they stopped them working on the farm and kept them working in one room dismantling telephones. What a soul destroying job!

Until 1958 the Mid Wales had supplied its own water and generated its own electricity. This self-sufficiency went too.

> When they went onto a different supply they had to put five times the amount of chlorine in to get the water back to the same standard it was before and build a big pumping station at Pengenffordd [to pump up a mains supply] whereas before it was all gravity fed. That's progress! So it was, dig up 20 miles of road instead of building a bigger dam across the Hospital part of the wood.

The Mental Health Act of 1959

There must have been a more substantial reason than political correctness for reducing the self-sufficiency of the Mid Wales Hospital by one means or another. There was, and it was presaged by the Mental Health Act of 1959 that replaced the old laws on lunacy. The main aim of the Act was to follow the therapeutic revolution in drugs by transferring as much treatment as possible to outpatient departments, thereby reducing the time spent in hospital. Ideally, treatment should be voluntary and informal; when there had to be compulsion, it should be within a proper legal framework. The result would be to move treatment out of institutional care and into the community, and reduce the stigma of mental illness. This meant the beginning of the end for the old asylums. For the time being much of this remained an aspiration.

What did become law, however, was the new definition of 'mental disorder'. The Act distinguished 'mental illness' from 'mental handicap'. Mental illness was given a loose definition, covering 'psychopathic disorder, and any other disorder or disability of mind'. It went on to define psychopathic disorder as 'a persistent disorder which results in abnormally aggressive or seriously irresponsible conduct' and this applied to psychotic states like schizophrenia. Mental handicap, formerly 'subnormality', was given a tighter definition as 'arrested or incomplete development of mind'. The Act went on to abolish the Mental Imbecility Act of 1913, so the pejorative words 'subnormal' and 'imbecile' were now banished from official terminology.

These definitions were all very well in theory; in practice, it was often difficult to distinguish between 'mental illness' and 'mental handicap', partly because some patients suffered from both. Monty Graham joined the Mid Wales as an assistant nurse in 1963, became Nursing Officer responsible for Community Mental Health Services in Powys (for which he was given the MBE) and ending as a Mental Health Commissioner for a further decade. So he speaks from experience:

> The Mid Wales in my day was not intended as a hospital for 'learning disability' patients or the 'mentally handicapped' as they were called then. But there's always been an argument about where mental illness stops and learning disabilities begin. When I was a Mental Health Commissioner I visited

all the hospitals for both categories from here to Lancaster and the whole of the West Midlands. There was always an argument because patients with learning disabilities on acute wards were always, or usually, very disruptive; and the psychiatrist would say, 'No, this isn't mental illness, this is a disability problem' and the consultant from disability would say, 'No, he's got a mental illness'. Neither wanted them, you see, because they were very difficult to look after. I can remember at least ten female patients at the Mid Wales who clearly, clearly had a mental illness but they were also clearly suffering from learning disabilities.

Two years later, in 1961, the Conservative Government made its first public commitment to phasing out the former asylums. This included, once again, a change of name. The word 'mental' was dropped so that the Mid Wales Mental Hospital became simply the 'Mid Wales'. The commitment came in the famous 'Water Tower' speech made by Minister

Minister of Health Enoch Powell, seated third from left visits Mid Wales Hospital in 1961

of Health Enoch Powell in March 1961, six months before he visited Talgarth. His arrival must have been rather like Daniel entering the lion's den, for his speech included a description that could have been of the Mid Wales Hospital, the former asylum he now wished to abolish:

> There they stand, isolated, majestic, imperious, brooded over by the gigantic water-tower and chimney combined, rising unmistakable and daunting out of the country-side – the asylums which our forefathers built with such immense solidity to express the notions of their day. Do not for a moment underestimate their powers of resistance to our assault. Let me describe some of the defences which we have to storm. First there is the actual physical solidity of the buildings themselves; the very idea of these monuments derelict or demolished arouses an instinctive resistance in the mind. Well, let me declare that if we err, it is our duty to err on the side of ruthlessness. For the great majority of these establishments there is no appropriate future use, and I for my own part will resist any attempt to foist another purpose upon them.

Enoch Powell had a vision. Owing to the therapeutic drug revolution, he foresaw that in fifteen years the number of mentally ill patients who required hospital care would be reduced by half, and they should be looked after in psychiatric units attached to general hospitals. He did not use the phrase 'community care' in his speech but that is what he intended for the remainder:

> That is why, at the earliest moment possible, I intend to call on local health and welfare services, through the bodies which represent them, to take a hand in mapping the joint future of the hospital and the local authority services.

Aerial view of the Mid Wales Hospital in 1961

Enoch Powell's 'vision' would take far more than fifteen years to materialise, but the winds of change would soon blow hard over the Welsh hills.

Chapter Four

In-Care, Out-Care

The General Nursing Council reported in March 1971 on its seventh visit to the Mid Wales Hospital since the founding of the NHS. This is the last report in the archives open to the public. It serves as an introduction to the Hospital as it entered its seventh decade, and began the last 30 years of its existence. The age-old problem is laid clear in one of the first sentences: 'There are ten wards for psychogeriatric and long-stay patients (six women, four men). There are two wards for disturbed patients and two admission wards'. In other words, only about 30 per cent at most of the 452 patients (those on the admission and disturbed wards) received treatment working towards their discharge. The 'Remarks' come as no surprise:

> The hospital is in very rural surroundings, 18 miles from the nearest rail station at Abergavenny. [Talgarth station closed in 1962.] Buses are infrequent. Most staff rely on own transport and have to pay the first 12 shillings per week. Not easy to recruit staff and many more nurses are required – several recruits from Mauritius has eased burden. Less than half the wards are constantly supervised at night.
>
> The proportion of elderly people living in the area is 50 per cent higher than the national average and this is reflected on the wards. Even on admission wards most patients have been there for over a year. Very few young patients are admitted. This is bad for nursing experience because there isn't another psychiatric hospital offering acute experience in the area. The time for teaching on the wards is limited by the increasing load of routine care placed upon nursing teams by an aging hospital population.

> The standard of patient care and hygiene is mostly satisfactory. There is a friendly atmosphere and spirit of co-operation. The wards appeared to be mostly pleasant and comfortable but more privacy should be given to the toilets where many doors are half length.

The report, then, could be summarised as 'doing pretty well in the circumstances' and this must have come as a relief because close by, in the world of mental hospitals, a huge scandal had recently been exposed that hammered another nail in the coffin of the old asylums. This was the exposure in the *News of the World* in 1967 of abuse, neglect, cruelty and pilfering at Ely Hospital in Cardiff. A Committee of Inquiry reported in 1969. It described an institution that was quite like the Mid Wales – except that Ely was officially for mentally handicapped patients as well as the mentally ill, whereas at the Mid Wales this combination existed but was not made explicit. According to a later Labour AM for Cardiff West, Mark Drakeford, in whose constituency Ely was situated:

> The picture which emerged was of an institution cut off professionally from the wider world of patient care. One part-time and two full-time doctors were responsible for the care of 660 patients. Doctors almost never ventured into the 'back' wards where the oldest and least able patients were gathered together. Some, who had originally been categorised as 'imbeciles', had been in Ely since before the Great War.

The report led to a Government paper in 1971 *Better Services for the Mentally Handicapped*. Mark Drakeford went further by saying that the closure of the old asylums advocated by Enoch Powell ten years earlier 'would not have gone ahead had it not been for Ely'. It is a tribute to the Mid Wales that the GNC report the same year – 1971 – gave it a clean bill of health.

Into the community

In 1974, the Mid Wales Hospital became the responsibility of Powys Area Health Authority and big administrative changes were in the pipeline.

Dr Diggle retired and afterwards the title of Medical Superintendent lapsed. Chancefield was converted into flats for staff. From then on the hospital was managed by the Secretary, the first being Gwyn Lewis, who was in post until Delcie Davies became Manager in 1983. When Dr Michael Hession was appointed as consultant psychiatrist in 1977 (in succession to the Polish consultant Dr Longin Dolny) he joined a team with Dr Mohan Bhakta and Dr Alan Phillips. They were appointed by the Health Authority and held responsibilities inside and outside the Mid Wales. In the hospital each had his own wards and acute admission beds; outside they ran outpatient clinics which developed into stand-alone community resource centres with full-time nursing and other staff. They divided the Powys area geographically. Dr Hession was responsible for Mid Powys (Llandrindod Wells, Builth Wells, Knighton and Rhayader), Dr Bhakta ran Brecon and Ystradgynlais, and Dr Phillips was in clinical charge of mental health for Newtown, Welshpool and Machynlleth – Welsh-speaking areas, so it made sense for these patients to be placed in the same wards.

The trouble was that Powys Health Authority, like its predecessors, covered a large area with a small population. The consultant team was away from the Mid Wales for perhaps two days a week. Nevill Hall hospital in Abergavenny opened in 1969 but it did not provide a psychiatric service and had little contact with the Mid Wales except for treating physically ill patients – and only then if a round-the-clock nurse accompanied the patient from the Mid Wales.

Thus within the Mid Wales the consultants held clinical authority while administrative authority rested with the Secretary. Dr Phillips soon retired, to be replaced by Dr Gareth Hughes, and when Dr Bhakta died in post in 1995 he was replaced by Dr Jonathan Hill. Dr Michael Hession became Senior Consultant with managerial committee functions in the

Mid Wales and also for Powys Health Authority. With these structural changes the move to community care, presaged by the 1959 Mental Health Act, was at last formally under way.

From the mid 1970s a network of mental health services was stretching out from the Mid Wales into the far reaches of Powys. Eight Community Psychiatric Nurses were appointed by Gerald McCarthy (see below) and placed in Ystradgynlais, Brecon, Builth, Llandrindod, Knighton, Llandiloes, Machynlleth, Welshpool and Newtown. These were attached to outpatient clinics which grew through the 1980s and early 90s into Mental Health Resource Centres in the main towns of Brecon, Llandrindod, Ystradgynlais, Newtown and Welshpool. The first Centre was 'The Hazels' in Llandrindod Wells which opened in 1980. Here was a multi-disciplinary team of a community psychiatric nurse, a psychologist (from the Mid Wales) and an occupational therapist. Each had a caseload of patients they would see at home, at the Centre or, when necessary, at the Mid Wales. The Centres were connected to general medical practices too, so that, for example, the Mid Wales nurse David Lewis in 1985 went out to work at Brecon Resource Centre with responsibility for a general practice at Hay-on-Wye. Money came from the Welsh Office, which showed that the political wind continued to blow hard towards the implementation of community care.

Institutionalisation

In 1973 Gerald McCarthy was appointed to the Mid Wales as Senior Nursing Officer. It was a controversial appointment and would continue to be so until he left ten years later. McCarthy came from Whitchurch Hospital in Cardiff and he looked on the Mid Wales through the eyes of an outsider. What was his first impression?

> Desperate! I'll tell you the truth of it. My first day in the office there was a letter on my desk from the GNC [General Nursing Council]. It told me that if I didn't improve the

clinical environment of the hospital then it would take the school off us. And that was the first day!

In my mind, we had been left so far behind. Every time you talked up something the nursing staff, who had grown up in the system, found an argument for not changing. It was all so traditional, right? What happened in the 1930s and 40s and 50s still happened in the 1970s.

Take privacy. The patients were basically regarded as pets. You looked after them, you fed them, you kept them clean, you ensured they were healthy, but what you didn't do was give them privacy and dignity. The so-called Nightingale wards, the open dormitories, were way out of date, and the term 'airing courts' should have been dropped long ago.

Now, the trouble was that if you grew up in that environment, you would say to me, 'There's nothing wrong with that. We're looking after the patients. We do the best we can for them'. And they were. There's no way they were cruel to patients. But from the government down, the professionals were asking, 'Can any of these patients fit into the community?' Right? Well, that did not even enter the staff's minds. Most of the patients were long-term – not because they needed to be long-term, but because that's how the system worked. The main emphasis was on containment, keeping things quiet. Once you were in with schizophrenia for example, you were in for a long, long time. It was the easiest thing to just leave people where they were, and so the years went by. I wish the patients had complained more but they didn't.

Pets are dependent on their masters and McCarthy went on to explain the culture of dependency which he said characterised patient-staff relations at the Mid Wales:

Say the staff took patients down to the pub, the ones who could walk the three-quarters of a mile into town. Now, the hard part was to get the staff to give the patients money to get their own drinks. The staff sat the patients down and got them the drinks. Everything was maintained on dependency. The same with occupational therapy. You would go up there and say, 'Can you make me a toy for my six-year old daughter?' And they said, 'Yes, we can do that'. But no patient would get involved. The staff would make it. The same with working in gardens outside the grounds, because I found some work there. The patients were always escorted. The Charges went with them.

Now one of the arguments always put against me is the question, 'What would the patients do at home that was different to what they're doing here?' But the difference was that they would be at home, they would be independent.

It was the isolation of Talgarth that made the nurses so set in their ways, McCarthy continued – that and the power of the trade unions in the 1970s. He said as an example that he advertised for an assistant charge nurse and he had ten or twelve applications, all from the local area and all giving as referee local worthies like the Talgarth grocer or butcher or newsagent. None had found referees who could give clinical references and were not working at the hospital: 'I was losing the battle, I think, because everyone was coming through the system and 90 per cent lived in the system, right?'

What this culture of dependency amounted to was institutionalisation. The *Cambridge English Dictionary* defines it simply as: 'If someone becomes institutionalised, they gradually become less able to think and act independently, because of having lived for a long time under the rules of an institution'. This mind set applies to so-called 'total institutions' such as prisons or mental hospitals, where inmates and to a lesser extent staff are inside that institution for years on end. Andrew Price, who was a nurse at the Mid Wales in the 1990s, described how institutionalisation affected patients at the time when their routine was disturbed as a result of the moves out into the community:

> Well, I don't know if you can understand, but even working at the Mid Wales for a long time you get a bit like it [institutionalised]. It's like the routine is so rigid every day and that's what you do. And if something that's supposed to happen doesn't happen, that's when people start getting really annoyed. The routine has got to happen every day, the same time throughout the day. You can't adjust to anything new, and if you are required to it can have damaging consequences.

Back in the 1970s, Joan Devereux had found it hard to accept the rigid regimentation that dominated the day on the wards:

> I became rather depressed about how regimented everything was. Patients had to have a bath on a certain day of the week, once a week. They had a laxative once a week whether they needed it or not. They had their hair combed with a small-tooth comb once a week. Their shoes were cleaned [by the nurses] once a week whether they needed it or not. We had a weekly dance every Wednesday, a Whist drive every Monday, weekly pictures [films] and weekly church service. We had a monthly walk with a nurse in front, the patients in some sort of crocodile, and a nurse bringing up the rear.
>
> You very quickly became institutionalised yourself. You started to fall in with it even if you couldn't see the point of it. Why did we do these awful things?

The worse thing was waiting outside Sister's door at 7.30 in the morning until you were invited in. You were preparing for the morning wash on the ward. You would collect a long bar of soap, a brass key to unlock the hot water on the hand basins and a plug. Soap, Key, Plug; Soap, Key, Plug, in that order. I'll never forget it.

Another former nurse said that on his ward at night the charge nurse insisted that he woke patients up to give them their sleeping pills. So routine became a rigid framework for the day and any change was resisted. Bill Devereux, perhaps speaking for the old school of nurses, supported it:

Institutionalisation became a dirty word. But when you were handling 50 or so patients you had to have law and order; you can't have 50 patients coming to breakfast any old time. You had to make sure they were clean and tidy even if it offended their civil liberty not to be. You see, for the long-term patients we were their family and the ward was their home: so we behaved like a family does.

Did we have pets? Oh, I think we did. We all had special patients we could rely on to do particular jobs, like counting the cutlery in the ward kitchen for example, or making the tea. That was their domain. They were 'Charge's batman' if you like: 'I'll put the laundry away, Charge, I've counted all the sheets and put X number in the 'condemned box'' [as needing to go to the stores to be replaced].

Andrew Price was once on the receiving end of a 'pet's' temper when she was guarding her territory:

I was a bit green when I went to the Mid Wales, a bit naïve. Everyone seemed to have their own job patient-wise, in the kitchen, sweeping up under the tables. I walked in to a ward kitchen one day and I moved something that I thought shouldn't have been there and I got slapped across the face by quite an elderly female patient. Yes, really, 'Bang!' because in her mind I was taking her job off her.

One of the sad results of institutionalisation at the Mid Wales was that some patients realised it was happening to them and could not do anything about it. They even had a local colloquialism to refer to it, as in the words of one ex-patient 'I've been f———g Talgarthed'.

What did the law say about the long term stay of patients in these 'back' wards? The Mental Health Act of 1959, more or less confirmed in 1983, was determined to protect the rights of patients who were detained in mental hospitals. When a patient was compulsorily committed, after approval by two specialist doctors, the hospital had 28 days to assess the case before application for release. If the recommendation was for continued detention then the patient had the right after six months to demand that a Mental Health Tribunal review the case. This review took place subsequently every three years (annually after 1983). Dr Michael Hession was clear that the law was obeyed:

The Hospital was meticulous in complying with the Mental Health Act (MHA) and the Mental Health Act Commission regarding the procedures and time limits for compulsory detention. In addition to Section 2 for 28 days and Section 3 for six months, there was an emergency section for 3 days and police transfer 'to a place of safety' [Section 136].

Very, very few patients on the long-stay wards were subject to detention under the MHA. I had four wards with 20–30 beds each, two male and two female; the ground floor wards were almost all occupied by elderly long-stay patients, none of whom, to the best of my memory, was subject to

compulsory admission or treatment. Again with failing
memory I can only recall two patients on the upstairs wards
who were under long-term compulsory detention, subject to
regular renewals, and automatic referral to a Mental Health
Review Tribunal if the patient or his family did not exercise
their right to ask for a Tribunal.

Most of these long-stay patients, then, had been referred to the Mid Wales
by their GP. They were voluntary patients and therefore the law had
nothing to say – although, as Dr Hession said, 'one might question how
voluntary was voluntary?'

Dr Hession referred to an incident about this time that showed how
difficult it was to expect elderly patients to leave when the catchment area
of the Mid Wales was so vast:

> In 1968 about 40 patients were transferred to the Mid Wales
> Hospital from Shelton Hospital, Shrewsbury, following the
> disastrous and tragic fire at Shelton. I 'inherited' maybe 20
> of these patients. They were all very old long-stay patients
> (mostly dual diagnosis – mental handicap and mental illness)
> at Shelton and were selected for transfer to MWH on the
> basis that they had no known relatives or an inactive family,
> and with no active links to a Shropshire community. There
> was no realistic prospect of rehabilitation to a community.
> They nearly all died during the first ten years of my tenure.

Opening the doors

Through the efforts of Dr Bhakta – who brought with him from
Whitchurch Hospital in Cardiff a progressive attitude to mental treatment
– and staff like Gerald McCarthy, Monty Graham and Keith Parry, in the
early 1970s the Mid Wales Hospital began to open up. The public was
made welcome. In 1971 the Mid Wales Horticultural Show attracted 430

Mid Wales Hospital Sports and Fete in the 1980s

entries. The next year the Mid Wales Hospital Sports and Fete was opened by the Chairman of the League of Friends; a carnival queen processed up from Talgarth on a float with page boys preceded by the Blackwood Girls' Band; there were stalls, children's races and a skittles competition. Talgarth children were invited to Christmas parties, Easter parades and sports days. Patrick Sharman, who joined the staff as a student nurse in 1977, remembers how he and other children were prepared for this:

> As children in the local primary school we would often hear patients from the hospital walking past the playground talking to themselves, laughing or crying inappropriately or shouting and swearing at nobody in particular. We were made aware that these people were not well and we should not tease them or take the mickey, but also to be a little wary of some. As children we attended many functions held at the hospital. Patients were always around and not locked away.

As ever, the problem of remoteness reduced the sort of sociability between hospital and community that would have been good for everybody. The *Western Mail* of 4 April 1976 ran a salutary article under the heading: 'The Day Dora Missed the Country Bus':

> Four years ago the only public transport service between Brecon and Newtown was withdrawn by the Crosville Bus Company. At about the same time 90-year old Mrs May Davies was admitted to the Mid Wales. Her 63-year old daughter, Mrs Dora Price, was left with a simple choice. She could either beg lifts or not visit her mother. The 90-mile round trip in a taxi was out of the question. The Mid Wales Hospital Welfare Officer used his vehicle but the round trip for all visitors in one day was to cover 150 miles, so Mrs Price was away from home between 10 am and 6 pm. Her son needed a half-day off work to take her to visit her mother in his car.
>
> A Welsh Hospital Board report in 1972 found that 27 per cent of rural hospital visitors had severe financial problems and 16 per cent had severe transport problems.

Within the hospital most of the wards were now unlocked, which was seen by carriers of The Key as a symbol of the new openness. Joan Devereux was one of the first to 'kick against the closed door', so to speak:

> Dr Bob Owen from North Wales came to work at the Mid Wales and he was more forward thinking than some. I was a Charge Nurse on a female ward then. We decided to leave the door to the ward unlocked; very quietly, without telling the patients at first. Our biggest worry was when the press got to hear about it and reporters came who always went away locking the door behind them. But I can't recall an

occasion ever when we had to go out looking for someone from that ward.

Dr Owen was a Medical Assistant who worked at the Mid Wales for many years looking after the long-stay wards.

In fact, some patients did wander off from the hospital, and in 1975 two of them, both suffering from Alzheimer's disease were found drowned, one in the river Ennig and the other in a brook bordering the hospital grounds. The resultant report recommended that elderly patients should be placed on the ground floor with their own garden within the airing courts. This tragedy had happened when the Mid Wales was short of staff but it shows that the locked ward had been partly for the safety of patients.

Gerald McCarthy was always keen to break down barriers that seemed to protect out-of-date practices. One of his controversial decisions was to rota male nurses to work on female wards and vice versa, as was standard in the NHS, he said. This was resisted at first, particularly by some female nurses who were worried about their safety and workload (literally, in some cases, because of the weight of male bedridden patients). Solicitors' letters were threatened if not exchanged. The young male nurses like Keith Parry enjoyed being mothered by elderly female patients, who made them tea. The fuss soon blew over. In the same spirit of mixing the sexes and opening the doors, McCarthy began a social club for patients. Here coffee and tea were on hand while patients played bingo, darts and pool or held discussion groups, all supervised by staff.

The long-stay wards

What was happening on the long-stay wards in the 1970s and 80s? For a start, the wards and sanitary annexes were upgraded to improve privacy and allow more dignity, which would have impressed the Visiting Committees of former years. Ward W1 was converted from dormitories into individual cubicles. Staff who worked on these wards deny the suggestion that the patients were physically cared for but otherwise ignored as patients – or, for that matter, as human beings. Dr Hession, for example, says that he undertook weekly ward rounds and each week three cases were selected for formal case conference reviews of treatment and a review of current and future care plans. Incidentally, the days had gone when nurses were expected to manage these wards without the case notes of patients, assuming that they existed.

Patrick Sharman went so far as to say that the 1970s brought in a new kind of nursing at the Mid Wales:

> I was involved in the evolution of a system of nursing that took the good practical care that patients experienced at the Mid Wales to another level of individual care for each patient – no sharing of clothes and wash facilities and more individual choice.

Brian Evans, who joined in 1962 with Monty Graham and Keith Parry, specialised in the nursing care of the elderly. Did he let his patients lie in bed all day or watch television?

> No, No! On E4 F (female) we had at least one 'activities nurse' who came on the wards. She was a girl from Bronllys, an arty-crafty person who got all the patients up and about. If they weren't in OT [Occupational Therapy], and we sent as many as possible to OT, then they would be doing handicrafts on the Ward.
>
> I got a kitchen started in a side room and once a week four to six patients would take it in turns to cook dinner. I'd go down with them to the Talgarth butcher and we'd choose the meat and prepare quite a decent meal.
>
> E2 was an elderly male ward where some of the patients had dementia but they weren't just left sitting. We would interact with them as much as we could.

E3 F actually had a 'reminiscence' room. We decked it out with old stuff purloined from here and there and used it to encourage patients to talk about the old days.

Every Christmas there was a competition for the best-decorated ward and that was taken very seriously.

One of his simple ideas was copied on other wards and should be more copied today:

> You know when you go into a nursing home today the patients are all sitting around watching TV? I wasn't going to have that. We arranged the chairs in the day room in small groups so that the patients faced each other. Those who wanted to watch TV would have to move to the corner where we put it.

The Hospital League of Friends went on to the wards to be sociable and answer any needs they could. Of course, the routine of these wards went on as before, with patients who could do so helping with cleaning (those 'bumpers' again) and serving food. Physical exercise was encouraged. As in the old days, it was 'coats and boots on' for walks in the airing courts and gardens.

The Occupational Therapy department started making Christmas bunting in September and decorated the main hall with streamers and a massive tree. On Christmas Day it was the venue for a huge party, which as many patients as possible attended. Patrick Sharman's description, in a memoir he wrote just after the closure of the Mid Wales, could have been taken from Charles Dickens:

> On Christmas Day staff would have made sure all patients had been bought presents (many did not have families) and the League of Friends would also have provided at least one

present for every patient.

The wards would be well-stocked with the usual Xmas goodies – sweets, fruit, cakes, drinks – soft and alcoholic and Xmas dinner was a big affair.

The tables would be laid out with placemats, Xmas crackers, table decorations and all the usual festive regalia.

The turkey would come from the main kitchen and the Charge nurse would carve the bird at the head of the gallery – like the head of a massive family. On many of the downstairs wards it is possible to see where the carving knives had been sharpened for the event as the window sills on the ward kitchens have been worn away into hollow indentations.

Is distance lending enchantment to the view? Has nostalgia been prompted by the forced closure of the hospital and the wretched condition of its ruin

Christmas on a male ward in the 1990s

today? Or was the Mid Wales a bit special among mental hospitals? All of the staff I have spoken to share this warm memory of the 1970s and 80s, however unpleasant some of their work had to be. One whose views must be taken seriously is a former student nurse at the Mid Wales who now occupies a senior university post in Mental Health; she wanted to talk anonymously. She trained for her RMN qualification at the Mid Wales in the early 1980s and returned to work as a staff nurse for three more years. During her training she went on 9 placements of 12 weeks each, most of them in long-stay wards. She considers that the physical care of patients at the Mid Wales was of a high standard, certainly compared with other psychiatric hospitals of which she had experience. Her policy at mealtimes was to place patients who were 'with it' round the same tables and encourage conversation. She remembers taking a few patients at a time down to The Bell pub and making sure they understood how money worked. In those wards she recalled that there were always a few patients who had specific tasks like serving tea or working in the ward kitchen. She confirmed that physiotherapy, behavioural therapy and occupational therapy were provided for those who would benefit from it.

This is not to say that visitors to the 'back' wards at the Mid Wales found it easy, particularly newcomers. In the early 1980s the writer Duncan Fallowell and his friend April Ashley, the celebrated 'Queen of Hay', called to see an elderly friend from Hay-on-Wye who had been admitted due to senility. Both remember long, gloomy corridors leading to the ward (one of the nurses I spoke to actually said there were bats flying about) and then, on entry, the odour of urine and patients wandering about being disturbingly 'tactile'.

Their friend upset them, though not as much as he upset himself, by repeating constantly, 'I shouldn't be here, I shouldn't be here'. April took this in her stride. She told me 'Duncan was a wimp. My friend Sarah Churchill [the actress and artist daughter of Sir Winston Churchill] told me "Never ever be condescending to those who are drunk or drugged", so I remembered this'.

One of the mental health social workers I spoke to had a very unpleasant experience in one of those gloomy corridors. As a trainee she had been given a placement at the Mid Wales and on her first day she encountered a young male patient wearing pyjamas advancing towards her along an otherwise empty corridor. There were no nurses to be seen. He badly sexually abused her and when she broke free and complained to the nurses on the nearest ward they laughed. I put this to Dr Michael Hession, whose reply was that he was sympathetic to the 'young lady' but 'I'm surprised this did not happen more often'. The Mid Wales was a mental hospital, he said, with men and women living in close proximity all the time, often not dressed. Nevertheless, he could honestly not recall any cases of sexual abuse, though he did recall several patient 'relationships'. Here the problem was an ethical one much more than a practical one. 'Relationships' between members of staff were much more common.

When Keith Parry became Manager in the 1990s he started a Patients' Council. At first, patient representatives met monthly with one or two charge nurses and Keith himself to discuss suggestions. One of the first was to unlock the ward kitchens so that patients could make themselves cups of tea. It went from there:

> In fact, for the first time patients were given a voice in the way ward routines and services were delivered. Patients became involved in negotiating changes to such things as the format of weekly case conferences, menus and meal times. The Patients' Council had direct access to me as the service manager.
>
> Then this led to the appointment of a Patients' Advocate who among other duties supported patients with complaints and matters relating to the Mental Health Act. I was very proud of that as we were one of the very few mental hospitals to do this.

Over the next two years patient representatives joined the voluntary groups participating in all aspects of the planning process for the decommissioning of the hospital and the re-provisioning of services after the Mid Wales closure. They became persistent and needed to be. They certainly made a difference.

Outings

A major innovation, much talked about today, was hospital outings and these included patients from the long-stay wards. Once again, Keith Parry proved to be an innovator when he had responsibility for rehabilitation and entertainment in the 1980s. He set up inter-hospital cricket matches, on one occasion with a mental hospital in Taunton. Arnold Weale took his Project Team to Fishguard where they worked on a farm and slept out-of-doors, enjoying eating rabbit shot by Arnold. Perhaps they were on their way to Ireland, because there is another memory of the Project Team, that of 10 patients and 5 nurses, travelling to Connemara, where they went cockling and were well received in the pubs of Roundstone. Ambition grew and soon parties of patients were staying at Butlins holiday camps. This was not an easy experience for the nurses, as Brian and Joan Devereux remember:

> *Brian:* It was a bit hairy at times. You were taking patients who had never been anywhere before really. They hadn't drunk alcohol. They came from farms where no one had these sorts of holidays. And they were mixing with the general public at Butlins, you know, going into the dining rooms. Some would play up and you'd see people looking, sort of smiling, but some with shock horror.
>
> *Joan:* Some patients had come in [to the Mid Wales] as young people and now they were retirement age. When they were young at home their families couldn't cope with their

behaviour and when they were in the hospital their behaviour wasn't seen as so extraordinary; it was more acceptable in that environment.

Brian: Yeh, and suddenly they'd find themselves in a dining room in Butlins! But it went very well in the end.

On one occasion Gerald MacCarthey with his wife and eldest daughter took a party of 36 patients to stay at Aberystwyth University during a vacation. He recalls an hilarious incident:

> We had one patient who had never ridden in a police car with the siren going. So he went down to the police station and asked for a lift. And when they took him back to the university other patients piled in and they went around with the siren going off!

Ken Bowen and his wife Janet, a State Enrolled Nurse at the Mid Wales, took a party of elderly ladies to stay at the Midlands Hotel in Bournemouth. They loved the music and dancing and were determined to make the most of it. Janet Bowen:

> My, it was hard work for me. They had borrowed the prettiest clothes they could get and they were going to dress to look pretty. Trouble was, they couldn't dress themselves or do their hair and they hadn't worn make up so I had to do it all, and wash them and their clothes.

The hospital staff ran very successful football and cricket teams. On away matches they took patients with them as a supporters' club, and insisted they share in the socialising afterwards, a practice not followed by other mental hospitals. At North Wales Hospital in Denbigh, for instance, the away fans were banned from the bar, so Mid Wales players and supporters

An outing with Donald Harris (back row second right) in the 1970s

jumped into the bus and went off to the Bridgend Inn in Wem (Shropshire), 50 miles away.

At weekends the Mid Wales provided a minibus service down to Talgarth. It was driven by the Head Porter, Ken Bowen, who managed a staff of twelve. Once again, the old days had gone when there were few porters and no vehicles. In fact, with an electrician, carpenter, painter, decorator and plumber on site the hospital was self-sufficient in its support services, if no longer for its supplies. Ken would bring back patients from Talgarth who had been drinking when they shouldn't have been, or had drunk too much. The landlady of The Bell, a favourite pub, would spot when a patient was wearing slippers and knew enough about the hospital to ring his ward (it was normally a male patient) and demand his collection.

Occasionally, Ken Bowen was called out to round up a patient who had absconded. One got as far as Builth Wells.

One of the porters' duties was to act as pallbearers, for this was no longer a job considered suitable for male nurses. Until Delcie Davies became Manager in 1983 deceased patients were simply laid out on a slab in the mortuary with a plastic pillow: that was all. She made sure there

Ken Bowen still holds on to his key

was a decent covered trolley to transport a body off the ward and equipped the mortuary with three freezer cabinets. She did her best to convert it into a Chapel of Rest.

Wards 7 and 8

Clinical work at the Mid Wales during this period was centred on the Admission Wards, that is Wards East 7 and East 8 in the so-called New Building. These were also the Acute Wards, meaning that the patients were suffering from severe symptoms of, for example, manic depression that

Ward E 7 in 2018, with observation window at the back

could be suicidal, or schizophrenia that could be violent, or drug abuse and alcoholism that had reached crisis point. Here the clinicians concentrated their work, if not to cure then to alleviate. About 25 per cent of patients were in a mental hospital for the first time, and a further 25 per cent came in on a Section. A few arrived in handcuffs or strapped to stretchers forcibly escorted by the police, and they were placed in side rooms.

The two wards held 48 beds altogether and most patients occupied them for between ten days and six weeks before being released back into the community or moved to another ward. Ward 8 was for the catchment area of Breconshire and came under Dr Bhakta; Ward 7 was for patients from Mid Powys and Montgomeryshire, which meant that treatment came under Dr Hession and Dr Phillips. The sexes were divided on the wards into male and female dormitories but mixed in the day and dining area.

Unsurprisingly, Wards 7 and 8 were not happy places. Sometimes they were in crisis because of a patient's violent behaviour and even had to be closed to newcomers. Dr Hession gave me one example. In the late 1980s a 'highly dangerous' patient was admitted after he had attacked his GP. The police demanded that the Mid Wales should accept him, although there were no padded cells then and little means of restraint. The staff on

Jean Morgan with her husband collects her MBE at the Palace

Ward 7 anticipated a 'potentially murderous situation', but over the next few days it was 'defused' by the Ward Sister, Jean Morgan. Showing courage and compassion she calmed him down, and for 'services to nursing' she was awarded the MBE. The patient spent several years in the hospital and became 'quite endearing'. He was a cartoonist and gave Dr Hession a drawing which neatly reversed the tables on the patient/consultant relationship.

Another patient on Ward 8, in 1979–1980, was a former officer in the Royal Regiment of Wales, Jonathan Morgan. He was suffering from post-traumatic stress as a result, initially, of being stationed with his regiment in Belfast at the height of the Troubles in 1972. His battalion suffered six deaths and 26 injured in a matter of months, and it was too much for him. He was 'near cracking point', so he was posted out early; by the time he had returned from a tour of duty in Belize, a few years later, he had 'almost gone mad'. He left the army but 'finally cracked' when he was found running down a London street without trousers, thinking he was in the middle of a nuclear war. He returned home to Brecon and became a voluntary patient in the Mid Wales, diagnosed as suffering from manic depressive psychosis.

He said entering the Mid Wales was like 'going into hell'. On Ward 7 he had no privacy and remembers the staff looking at him through a thick glass observation panel. Being all too aware that he was 'a broken man', he felt his 'madness was accentuated' by being with patients who were just as ill, or more ill, than he was. He was lonely and scared, but found solace sitting in the waiting room in the new Treatment Block where there was an uninterrupted view over the 'lovely mountains'.

Jonathan Morgan says he was 'disturbed by supernatural struggles' and what the Old Testament calls 'demons'. To him, the chapel at the Mid Wales was 'possessed by the devil', a place of 'black magic'. He was saved, he writes in a published book in which he refers to himself in the third person, by a psychotic dream in which:

'Psycho' Michael Hession, a patient's cartoon

'Psycho' Hession again, by the same patient

He was taken to a high altar by a godfather figure called Bishop Lucy who had haunted the chapel of his old school at Christ College [Brecon]. He was given communion by a presence he dared not look at but, from that time on, he started to recover.

'I had been in the presence of the Good Lord', he told me. More practically, he was given an anti-psychotic tranquilliser called Stelazine by Dr Bhakta, and after these two experiences he began to recover.

What he did not get was any group or one-to-one therapy. Sister Morgan, he says, was caring but 'an old-fashioned matron'; Bhakta was 'distant'. There was no therapeutic interaction encouraged between patients and the closest he got was self-therapy by walking in the 'lovely countryside'.

I put this criticism to a former nurse, Patrick Sharman, who had knowledge of Wards 7 and 8. He agreed that treatment was on the medical model and that was the historic experience at the Mid Wales up to that time. It was, however, in the process of change with the arrival of behavioural and psychotherapy (see below). Further, he said, these wards were unhappy places because the quick turnover of patients was unsettling and prevented the sort of social bonding on the long-stay wards. There is more to add.

First, another criticism from this period of the early to mid 80s: the mental health social worker referred to earlier (who wishes to remain anonymous) had to escort sectioned patients to Wards 7 and 8. She remembers the dread as the ambulance drove up 'that lonely hill bordered by old iron railings and through the gates, past that Dickensian building – Bleak House it should be called – to Wards 7 and 8'. On arrival, she said, if the patient was sectioned he would be 'whacked up with Largactil' to keep him quiet. There was little empathy from the nurses, she said, little information given to a bewildered and frightened newcomer like 'What would happen to his clothes? When could he have visitors?' She found the ward 'intimidating'.

It so happens that the student nurse quoted earlier who is now a senior academic was on '7s and 8s' during this period, so I put these criticisms to her. She said that her RMN training at the Mid Wales emphasised 'treating patients with respect', and she had followed this throughout her career. She certainly found these wards 'challenging'. At the core of her work was risk assessment. The patients were constantly under watch from the time they had their possessions searched on arrival for dangerous weapons or drugs. Some patients had been removed to the Mid Wales as a 'place of safety' under the Mental Health Act, and this meant *their* safety as well as the safety of those around them. They were told their rights under the Mental Health Act and their cases were constantly under review by the multi-disciplinary team.

All this is confirmed by Dr Hession. These were difficult wards, he said, but no more so than at any mental hospital. He had every sympathy with the staff, who were sometimes in a state of crisis themselves: one minute confronting a potentially violent new patient, another minute going on a search party to find a patient who had absconded. Once again he praised the Ward Sister, Jean Morgan. As for therapeutic treatment, he could not speak for Bhakta's ward (8) but he certainly tried psychotherapy when it was appropriate (see below), though this was more part of ongoing treatment when the patient had moved off the acute ward.

Another student nurse who worked on these wards in the late 1970s was Phil Luffman, now a psychotherapist working in Carmarthen. After training, he left the Mid Wales to work at the Hazels Centre in Llandrindod Wells before returning as a charge nurse in 1990. Looking back, he said, the physical care was of a high standard, but where did progressive treatment come in? The treatment he gave, pushing his pills trolley round the wards, was definitely drug-based; there was no group psychotherapy, though there were 'pockets of creative initiative'; and he remembered the 'inspirational' Donald Harris in his Behaviour Therapy Unit (see below). As far as treatment went, he said, the Mid-Wales was a 'backwater'.

One patient in and out of Ward 8 between 1988 and 1997 was Phil Pashley, who has made a name for himself locally as a performing poet:

Ward East Eight

It was just like a prison without a lock on the door
A plain green carpet covered a concrete floor
The views were nice, the food was OK
Like some before me I could have run away
But that wasn't for me, I served my time
To think overloading the brain was my only crime.

The weekly case conference, taken by Dr Hill, left its mark on Phil:

Weekly Case Conference

I walked into the room
Wondered if my face would fit
I saw people who'd been good to me
Others who'd treated me like s**t
(Well that's what I thought at the time)
The psychiatrist spoke gently
His voice sounding like a friend
He said we've discussed you Phil
You are far too ill to go home this weekend
At times like this your knees go weak
At times like this it's solitude you seek
At times like this your future seems bleak
His final words see you, same time, next week

There were quite a number of young drug abusers on these wards and Phil remembers that they would feed their anti-psychotic drugs to a cat that had taken up residence.

In fact, from the late 1970s there was more therapeutic treatment on offer at the Mid Wales compared to before. The 'In care, Out care' hybrid lent itself to the new emphasis on behavioural therapy, psychotherapy and genuine occupational therapy. Once again, the seminal figures were Drs Bhakta and Hession, with the new cadre of senior nurses backing them up, including a remarkable former nurse who revolutionised Occupational Therapy: Mary Fenlon.

Behavioural therapy

In 1975, Dr Bhakta turned the old farm ward into a residential Behavioural Therapy Unit for ten or so patients; it became known as Tegfan. This was a major step in the new proactive approach to rehabilitation. Monty Graham was a charge nurse at the time and responsive to the question 'Why are we bringing people in the whole time, why don't we keep them out?' He joined with Dr Bhakta in determining to make the unit part of the integrated community service that was being put into place. Much of the treatment took place in outpatient clinics and at home; when patients were referred to the Mid Wales they sometimes would arrive directly at the Behavioural Unit, where case conferences were held involving community nurses as well as those at the Hospital.

'Behavioural therapy' was a buzz-word at the time, an umbrella term for types of therapy that treated anxiety-neurotic disorders like phobias and obsessive-compulsive behaviour. Obsessive Compulsive Disorder (OCD) is an anxiety that lurks in many of our minds in a mild way. For example, 'Did I turn off the lights before I left the house?' is an anxiety. It becomes an Obsession when the question nags us all the way to work. It becomes a Compulsion when you feel you have no alternative but to turn around and go home to check. This becomes a clinical case for treatment when you repeat this several times on the same day.

Under this umbrella too came sexual 'disorders' such as homosexuality, which was treated at several mental hospitals in the 1960s and 70s, but never at the Mid Wales. Behaviour therapy functions on the idea that all behaviours are learned so that unhealthy behaviour can be unlearned by a stick and carrot approach, or to put it more clinically, aversion and reward techniques.

Many patients must always have been grateful to the saintly nurse Donald Harris, an inspiring and self-taught believer in behavioural therapy. He used the stick and carrot in a common-sense way but always with compassion that seemed to win the trust of patients. He started nursing at the Mid Wales in 1958 and soon after he noticed that the sister of one of his friends had a complete aversion to having her hair cut; she just refused to go, so that she was frog-marched to the hairdressers and given a 'pudding-basin' haircut:

> I thought, well, I'll get her to want to go. So that was my start. I used to take her and reward her with chocolate, first if she entered the door, then if she sat in the chair and then when her hair was done. Chocolate was her reward and she was happy. She was vain, you see, she liked having her hair done well.

No-one else can have applied such a common-sense approach but then had the opportunity of developing it into a therapeutic tool in a mental hospital. Eventually, Donald was invited to the Maudsley Hospital, the most renowned psychiatric hospital in the UK, to give a lecture on his work.

When he started at Tegfan his aim was absolutely basic. He wanted to teach institutionalised patients how to wash and dress and then eat in public:

> The trouble with the Mid Wales was institutionalisation. My aim was getting people back into the community. There was no way they would ever survive outside. When you took

someone in the unit out for a meal it could be an embarrassment. I remember a landlady in one pub saying, 'Sorry, I don't serve patients'. I saw her point. For example, one of the patients would straight away go round and pick up all the fag ends from the ashtrays, which he would then hide away in his clothes.

The patients were so dependent, you see. They did nothing for themselves. They waited for nurses to do it: washing, shaving, dressing. They were incapable of functioning as individuals.

So the unit became a new home. The patients helped pay for the furnishings. Eventually they cooked simple meals and chose new clothes. They were made to cope by themselves with rewards of small sums of money and trips out to the pub; punishments meant staying in at Tegfan. Donald believed in patients having their say and out of that grew group therapy sessions.

Donald witnessed chronic obsessive-compulsive disorder which he couldn't even put a name to at first. 'We had a young girl referred to the unit, she was pulling her hair out. One side of her head was completely bald. What was the word? Trichotillomania it's called'. (Perhaps she was obsessed that she had lice in her hair and the compulsion was to remove them by tearing her hair out.) A most common form of OCD is repetitive hand-washing until the hands are raw. Whatever the psychiatric reasons for it, Donald was concerned how to stop it:

> I went to see a young girl who would take about three hours to have a bath. She just washed herself obsessively. I went once a week and set her little targets, like what to do with her hands. She had to make us a cup of tea in a very short time and then we'd have a chat. We often did that. This particular day I wanted her to have a bath so I brought a

timer with me and I set it for twenty minutes. I said 'I want you out of the bath and having a cup of tea with me before the timer goes off'. And she said 'There's no way I can do that. What happens if I can't do it?' I said 'I'll come in and get you out of the bath!' It worked.

Was it Donald's stick and carrot or his kindness and obvious affection for these afflicted people? He treated many phobias in this way:

There was this woman with bird phobia [Ornithophobia]. Oh, dear God! If she wanted to go shopping she would go on the bridge and watch the swans flying up and down the river. And the state she'd get in, dear God! Anxiety be damned! I treated it by desensitisation, it's called. [Dictionary definition 'diminished emotional responsiveness to a negative, aversive or positive stimulus after repeated exposure to it'.] I took her to a canal first with birds on it and we'd walk up and down, up and down. She was terrified at first, but she calmed down; then we went back to the bridge over the river. It worked.

Donald tried aversion therapy for alcoholics but that never worked. First he tried Antabus, a drug that reacts with alcohol to induce violent sickness and then, when that did not deter the alcoholic: 'We would connect the fingers of the chap to electrodes. We had a miniature bar and if he went for a soft drink that was OK, but if he went for a beer he'd get a shock. It was pretty uncomfortable, but it didn't really stop him drinking'.

Donald Harris found it difficult to recall some of his patients without becoming emotional. There was one memory that reduced him to tears:

Sometimes horrendous things happened. When I was at the outpatients at Ystradgynlais I used to hold group therapy. One of the women who came had a husband who gambled. One day she was very distressed so I asked her what had happened? 'I can't tell you, I feel ashamed'.

And I said 'You can tell me'. Her husband had gambled away his lorry which was his livelihood, and the bungalow. That's it, and all the money they had in the bank.

She said 'You must think terrible of me' and I said 'It's not your fault'. It was very distressing... Mind she... she didn't need any treatment. It was her husband who needed it.

But the group therapy helped a lot because it was a support network and if you lived in a remote place you needed to know there were people you could turn to. It was the opposite of institutionalisation.

Incidentally, although Harris had a way with his female patients, he was not at all at ease with Matron Mawr:

She was one of the old school. Terrifying! She was a stickler for her authority. I walked into her office once without being asked. 'What are you doing in my room?'
I said 'Do you mind a gentleman being here?'
And she said 'If you were a gentleman you wouldn't be in here'.

The Behaviour Therapy Unit became more sophisticated. The Mid Wales psychologist, John Wilkinson, introduced video interviews with role-playing to familiarise patients with life outside; and then it came to an end. Donald retired in 1985. His empirical approach of the stick and carrot, supported by his deeply compassionate nature, was replaced eventually by a small amount of cognitive behavioural therapy, an altogether more theoretical approach. In the meantime, behavioural therapy faded away from the Mid Wales. Tegfan remained open but was used as a rehabilitation 'half-way house'.

Psychotherapy

Over in the Admissions Wards and at Llandrindod Mental Health Centre, Dr Michael Hession was treating alcoholism in a very different way, from the perspective of a psychotherapist.

This is how he defined his work:

> It is using psychological methods to explore the meaning and reason that lay behind any emotional experience. Emotions don't arise capriciously or at random. The core of the casework is trying to understand the reasons behind them, most of them subconscious. When these subconscious mechanisms are brought to the surface the patient can deal with them in a more appropriate way. So psychotherapy and behavioural therapy start from different ends; the former is concerned with underlying meaning and the latter with observable experience.

Treating alcoholics was a good example:

> In the majority of cases alcohol was self-administered medication. There were underlying mental health issues like feelings of anxiety, panic, anger. By turning to alcohol they suppressed the issues they could not deal with otherwise. I never bought into the theory that people drank a pint, then it was 2 pints, then over 10 years it was up to 8 pints – I don't think it happens that way. Physical dependence just through casual drinking rarely happens.

My approach was to take the alcoholic into Admissions, put him on the drug called Antabus containing disulfiram which, if you take alcohol on top of it, produces an extremely nauseous reaction and a drop in blood pressure. This scares the living daylights out of the alcoholic. Even if he refuses to continue on Antabus it takes several days before he can start drinking again as he has to get the drug out of his system. That gives us some days to start working on some of the issues. Very often they are family issues, often requiring to get some of the family in and start working, perhaps as a couple, linking what issue the person is trying to escape from – and then explore alternative ways, other than knocking them on the head with a bottle of whisky.

There were always two or three alcoholics on the Admission wards. There were anorexics too, who could be the presenting problem of a family issue:

Mother: 'Sylvia, Sylvia, do eat up your food'.
Daughter: 'I hate Daddy's guts'.

The dynamics of anorexia, said Hession, were all about control: refusal to eat could be a form of protest against parental authority. For this reason, the psychologist at the Mid Wales, John Wilkinson, would sometimes eat with the family at home to observe this dynamic. Part of his job was to take psychological measurements of intelligence or of personality, for example, so he was also called in to watch the weight of the anorexic. Below 35 kilos more drastic treatment than psychotherapy was required. Some severe anorexics verged on the psychotic, too, because they suffered from a distortion of body image. They saw themselves in a way that could be delusional or hallucinatory and here anti-psychotic medicine replaced psychotherapy.

The same was true in the Mother and Baby Unit that Dr Hession opened in two suites off Ward 7. One reason for post-natal depression could be environmental; taking the stress out of the mother by removing her to a safe and supportive place was enough to bring about recovery. But a few of his patients suffered from puerperal depression, an altogether more dangerous state because it could lead to self-harm or even infanticide. It is a post-natal psychosis where delusions and hallucinations can perceive the baby to be, in Dr Hession's experience at the Mid Wales, the offspring of 'a man of the forest', or 'the devil'. Once again, psychotherapy had nothing to offer and because the wards were unlocked constant supervision was necessary.

Michael Hession had the reputation for encouraging the progressive movement in psychiatry that from the 1960s attempted to 'decarcerate' the old asylums by experiments in setting up therapeutic communities outside. This was the beginnings of 'community care'. A good example of this was Dr Hession's invitation to the Mid Wales of the mental patient and artist, Mary Barnes.

In 1960 the Scottish psychiatrist R D Laing wrote *The Divided Self: an Existential Study in Sanity and Madness* which made a seminal impact by challenging the boundaries between sanity and insanity. He followed this by setting up Kingsley Hall in the East End of London which was an open, permissive community where patients worked through their illness with radical therapies. One patient there was Mary Barnes, a schizophrenic who underwent regressive therapy that took her back to her childhood. Under this influence she painted the walls of her room with her own faeces until she was given paints. Eventually she became a well-known painter, particularly of religious themes, and 'an ambassador of R D Laing'. She toured the country exhibiting her art and spreading the message of Laing by describing his teaching and the life at Kingsley Hall. Around 1980, Dr Hession invited her to the Mid Wales where she spoke to a group of psychiatrists and nurses. One of them was Phil Luffman who thought how

Snow *by Mary Barnes*

extraordinary it was to be addressed by a patient of R D Laing. She gave him one of her art works titled *Snow*.

Mary Barnes was never cured of schizophrenia, though she lived in a small Scottish village for the last years of her life, and these early experiments in self-standing therapeutic communities were only partially successful. It was said that they replaced the 'warehousing' of the old asylums with the 'revolving door' of psychiatric hospitals. In those areas where they were set up the numbers of patients in mental hospitals declined markedly, which would have pleased Enoch Powell, but the number of psychiatric admissions increased. It was largely a change in 'throughput'.

Occupational therapy
A major push towards 'positive rehabilitation' – another buzz-phrase – was the new Occupational Therapy Department opened in 1971, with places for 134 patients. This concrete barn-like structure with a corrugated roof

is located behind the shrubbery on the right after you enter the main gates of the Mid Wales; it replaced the old OT building that then became the Nurses' Training School. The new department was run by a professional Occupation Therapist, Mrs Mary Fenlon, who appointed Keith Parry as her deputy. The aim was to have less of the keeping occupied and more of the therapy. Mary Fenlon, by all accounts, was another of those formidable women – Matron Mary Mawr, Manager Delcie Davies – who left their mark on the history of the Mid Wales. She was a challenger of bureaucracy, an enemy of the 'staff comfort-zone', as she perceived it, and a dynamic believer in patient rehabilitation.

She kept some of the traditional OT like crochet, basketry and embroidery for female patients, but the much derided dismantling of telephones was out and industrial therapy was in. Parry negotiated one contract for the assembling and packaging of plastic toys like pedal tractors and cars, another contract for the making of concrete garden ornaments like gnomes and animals, a third for the stripping of yarn from damaged spindles used in the textile industry; these arrived by the lorry-load, were stripped, re-boxed and returned to the factory. 'The big thing,' said Parry, 'was that for the first time patients actually got paid; they could earn up to £10 a week, which could have been more but it was kept below the threshold of claiming for the Disability Living Allowance'.

At the end of the OT Department was the carpentry workshop run by Vernon Argent. He worked with inpatients, and outpatients who arrived by minibus; there was room in his workshop for about six at a time. Many had worked on farms and were good with their hands so that before long the workshop had full order books for a range of woodwork-like rustic furniture, bookcases, stools and picture framing, all sold below the market price. Vernon denied Gerald McCarthy's criticism that the skilled carpentry was done by the staff. He graded the work according to the skill of the patient. When making rustic furniture, for example, he allotted work from simply stripping the bark off branches to quite complex joinery and working with a lathe. 'It was the happiest time of my life, actually. I got on well with the patients. There was one guy with a great sense of humour, I remember. He went around singing the Ian Dury hit song 'It's Nice to be a Lunatic'.

It was the same up the road at Gwernllwyd Farm where Arnold Weale took his Project Team to pick potatoes and clear the fields of stones. Farmer Roy Thomas enjoyed working with them, found them no trouble, and remembers one with a similarly light-hearted attitude to his illness:

> He was a big guy from a farm in Montgomeryshire – I wouldn't have wanted to get on the wrong side of him – and a terrific worker. He said to me one day 'Mr Thomas, I could have been a rich man by now, like you. I could have had a farm too but they took it away from me when I was 21 because I went f*****g bonkers.'

Project Team hedge laying

The Project Team, incidentally, now lived together in Honddu House, the former Isolation Unit. Up in the market garden, horticultural therapy was provided by the making of window boxes, sowing seed, potting on and growing flowers.

Mary Fenlon's ambition to rehabilitate extended to the arts. She arranged for the Workers' Education Association to send history and drama teachers; one course was in creative writing, so that at Christmas and Easter the OT patients performed plays based on Bible stories. Perhaps to encourage a little intimate meeting of the sexes, she started cookery classes that culminated in two or three cooks (mostly female) inviting two or three guests (mostly male) to sit around the table and enjoy the results. All this was in the 1970s, remember. Her legacy was the saying 'don't do things *to* the patients, or *for* the patients, but *with* the patients'.

The Powys School of Nursing

Vernon Argent describes how his carpentry workshop was enlivened by student nurses who came there as part of their training. When Malcolm Dodds became Senior Tutor in Sole Charge of the School of Nursing in 1981 there were 60 students, 20 in each of three years, and the greater part of their time, as before, was spent gaining practical experience. The School had grown so that the Hospital now had the pick of the students it wanted to keep. Several RMNs from this period said that Malcolm Dodds was 'a breath of fresh air' and the training given was 'superb'.

The School now had its own Education Centre based in the former bakery which, with the butchery and tailors, had been closed down in the 1960s. The Centre incorporated a substantial library containing about 4,000 books, mostly of psychoanalytical or psychiatric specialism. Dr Hession built this up with the intention of gaining certification for teaching from the Royal College of Psychiatry. He was successful: so a Post-Basic Education Department offered training for junior doctors specialising in psychiatry who required an M.R.C. Psych. before becoming Senior House Doctors or Registrars. Dr Hession ran this course, normally attracting three or four post-graduates, some of whom lived in Chancefield House. The Department also laid on courses in community care, including one for general practitioners.

All this came to an end in 1992 when nursing education moved into higher education. The Powys School of Nursing merged with two other Schools of Nursing and reappeared at Swansea University, where Malcolm Dodds himself moved. Thus the Mid Wales lost its enthusiastic organiser of entertainments for patients and public, and a principal actor too.

It is a sad irony that just when the Mid Wales Hospital was keeping pace with the modern requirements of mental health care it failed to achieve the one thing that mattered, which was to prevent its own closure. In the face of long-standing government policy for community care, could it have done more? That is an argument still heard in the pubs of Talgarth.

Malcolm Dodds (Innkeeper) with his cast on the Mid Wales stage

Chapter Five

Closure

It is worth recalling at this stage how important the Mid Wales Hospital was to the small town of Talgarth. For a start it was the main employer and had been for several generations. Patrick Sharman is now manager of a 'supported living' hostel in Talgarth called Ashburnham House. He started at the Mid Wales as a student nurse in 1974 and his family was a case in point:

> My mother trained as an RMN [Registered Mental Nurse] in the 1950s, as did my older brother (1970s), two aunts – one RMN (she was awarded an OBE for services to nursing) one SEN [State Enrolled Nurse], two sisters-in-law (RMN and SEN) and several cousins (nurses and ancillary/domestic staff) have all worked there, as did my future wife in Occupational Therapy.
>
> This was a common factor for most families living in the Talgarth area. You either worked in the MWH, Bronllys Hospital, the Local Health Authority (main offices attached to Bronllys Hospital), with the County Council, or on a farm.

Even in the 1970s the Mid Wales Hospital was an institution with a vast workforce that allowed it to be self-sufficient in many ways. In this memoir about the Mid Wales that he wrote after its closure, Sharman estimated the size to be 300 people, almost as many staff then as there were patients:

> This was not just nurses and student nurses but medical staff, nurse tutors, administrators, secretaries, domestics, laundry, tailors/seamstresses, ground staff, artisans (electricians,

New Year Staff Ball in the Recreation Hall in 1970s

engineers, plumbers, carpenters, painters/decorators, stone masons), porters, cooks, canteen staff, kitchen staff, occupational therapy staff, psychologists, gardeners and store/supplies staff.

On reflection the list was seemingly endless as this place was a very self-contained, self-sufficient unit that ran as a small town may have done. For many staff it was a job for life – many retired after 40–50 years' service.

The Mid Wales had a mutually beneficial relationship with the town beyond. Most of the staff lived in Talgarth, shopped, drank and educated their children in Talgarth. The patients shopped and drank too, and it was more than that:

It was possible for people to gain apprenticeships for most trades within the hospital and this ensured not only a constant supply of employment to the local town but also

Recreation Hall in 2018

good access for local people to qualified tradesmen and opportunities for those tradesmen to branch out independently from the hospital if they wanted to.

According to Patrick Sharman and others, up until the mid 1980s few in the town considered that this relationship would end. Those who knew that community care was on the way and that there was a call for Victorian institutions to be closed down comforted themselves with two thoughts – 'It won't happen here because our standards of care are high', and 'There is nowhere else for the patients to go': long-stay patients still required hospital care and short-stay patients needed the specialist treatment that only the Mid Wales provided. This was the view of the local MP Richard Livsey, who said in 1984:

> Community care is only one parameter. The Mid Wales is doing a superb job for the rehabilitation of those suffering severe mental illness. This cannot be replicated elsewhere.

There is quite clearly a sound future for the Mid Wales Hospital.

Many staff at the hospital, isolated as ever from the world outside, thought the same. They were wrong. Others did see the straws in the wind and, like Monty Graham and David Lewis, moved out into community care.

Countdown

On 1 January 1984 Delcie Davies returned to the Mid Wales Hospital as first Secretary and then Manager with an annual budget of over £4m. She found a very different hospital from the one she had joined as a secretary in 1948: 'Totally different, totally different. Most wards weren't locked, there was a nice atmosphere, the student nurses were a breath of fresh air, the sexes mixed more and there was much more treatment'. Delcie had previously worked for Powys Health Authority so she was an insider, and she meant business. In particular, she was going to keep within budget. One of her first decisions that same year was to move out patients with 'learning disabilities' to spare beds at Bronllys Hospital, and Llys Maldwyn Hospital at Caersws, near Newtown. This was the first step in reducing patient numbers. That year the number of occupied beds at the Mid Wales fell to 283.

The first ward closed in 1989, the same year as the publication of the *All Wales Mental Illness Strategy* that confirmed the move to community care. By this time there were inpatient services for EMIs, as they were now called (Elderly Mentally Ill), at Ystradgynlais Community hospital, Ysbyty Gymuned Bro Ddyfi Hospital at Machynlleth, the War Memorial Hospital in Brecon and at Bronllys. More would soon be on the way at Llandrindod Wells, Welshpool and Newtown, all attached to Mental Health Resource Centres and Day Care services. This fitted the ambition of Powys Health Authority that 80 per cent of EMIs should be within 30 minutes' travel time of their homes. So, in theory anyway, patients who in the past might have ended their days at the Mid Wales would be hospitalised nearer their homes in these community hospitals.

Further, of course, there was 'natural wastage', the euphemistic phrase for patients who died in hospital. In 1994, when the number of patients in the Mid Wales had been reduced to 132, 88 of them were over 65 and 62 of these were over 75, so it is reasonable to assume that the death rate per year was at least what it always had been, that is roughly 8 per cent. It was most probably higher than that because the very act of moving old and institutionalised patients out of their wards could hasten their deaths. None of these vacated beds was occupied again.

Of course, owing to the advances in help for the mentally ill, both by drugs and psychiatric treatment, more patients were receiving day care while living at home. Further, the 'stepping stone' hostels in the grounds of the Mid Wales, Tegfan, Hillcrest and Honddu House, proved that patients could cope for themselves outside with some help. This led to a new development. Powys Health Authority said it would purchase residential mental health care by subsidising independent nursing homes and the first two of these in Talgarth were set up by former staff of the Mid Wales at Brenton Hall (the old vicarage) and Upper Lion (a former pub).

This was a stressful time at the Mid Wales. Delcie Davies was determined to reduce numbers, partly for financial reasons. She kept a chart in her office:

Oh yes, I'm a great believer in charts, charting the movement of patients in and out. I well remember Michael Hession coming in and asking 'What have you got there?' I told him: 'My intention is to close a ward because if I do so I will save £100,000' [which she needed to do to keep within a reducing budget]. Michael was horrified I was closing a ward. He said to me 'You close this ward and move patients and they will die. You will be responsible'. We moved the patients; we never lost one. You see, the numbers were dropping so it made sense to reduce the size.

In fact, in the 1990s when complete closure of the Mid Wales became a real possibility, both Delcie Davies and Michael Hession fought hard to keep it open. Another cause of friction was the conviction that those owners of the new independent nursing homes who had worked at the Mid Wales were returning to 'cherry pick' the patients they most wanted to look after. This was certainly Patrick Sharman's view (though a personal one, he hastens to say), and he should know because he is now the Manager of Ashburnham House, one of the remaining Residential and Care homes in Talgarth. It was also a worry of Phil Pashley. He was now on the Patients' Council and as such a member of a volunteer group participating in the de-commissioning process. He remembers making the point that former staff from the Mid Wales were setting up nursing homes without, it seemed, any background in the managerial skills required.

As the pace towards the decommissioning of the Mid Wales picked up through the 1980s, some staff and ex-staff complained bitterly that patients were virtually being chucked out onto the street. Bill Devereux, who retired in 1990, and his wife Sylvia, who retired three years later, were both strongly critical:

> *Bill*: We all knew it wasn't going to work. They were trying to send patients into nursing homes just so they could close wards.
>
> For example, at the hospital all the patients were visited by a doctor morning, afternoon and evening. The drugs were given at a certain time so every patient knew their drugs and when they must take them. [That didn't happen after they were discharged.] A sad joke about the community was two doctors talking to one another: 'We can discharge someone tomorrow if there's an empty park bench' – because where will they end up? On the street because they don't take their drugs!

Sylvia: Oh my God, I opposed it!

I can think of one patient, mentally handicapped she was, and I was sitting talking to her and she came from Newtown somewhere. She'd been passed to us because she was too hard to handle. She was at the Mid Wales all the time I was there [that is, since the 1950s] and she never saw her parents again. They couldn't visit her. Well, it came the time to discharge patients and they were going to send her back… I said, 'My God, you can't. That's worse than what they did to her when she was a child'.

Bill: This was her home and she only knew Talgarth, and they wanted to return her fifty miles away where she knew no one.

Sylvia: But you see, people in offices don't know these things, and if you tell them they don't listen. Well, they did listen, but she died.

Another accusation still heard in the pubs in Talgarth is that decommissioning the Mid Wales in the manner decided was a plot by Margaret Thatcher. She knew that moving elderly and sick patients around would precipitate their deaths and she encouraged it. This, of course, is without foundation but it shows the bitter feeling.

Probably the last therapeutic initiative at the Mid Wales was the appointment in 1990 of young Tessa Waite as Artist in Residence. She came for six months initially with funding from the South East Wales Arts Association, and she stayed for four years. She was given an empty ward, E6, and allowed to turn it into a studio. She had never worked in a mental hospital before and she found it 'a baptism of fire, a bit scary'. She sensed a powerful atmosphere of 'depression and suffering' amidst this tranquil landscape and she was aware, too, of the 'co-dependency' between staff and patients. Many had been for years in this total institution, each dependent on the other for getting through the day.

At first she felt at risk working in this big empty ward virtually on her own. Although attached to the Occupational Therapy Unit, she was given no health and safety advice nor supervision. However, in all the four years she was at the Mid Wales she experienced no sexual abuse. The nearest she came was when a male patient visited her studio and insisted on painting a portrait of her as though she were lying naked on a sofa – this was in his imagination, of course. She soon got used to patients coming to her studio with their 'odd behaviour, wild stories and depression'. She learnt to 'just be myself and accept that although I could not put distress to rights, I could be a positive influence'. In fact, the Mid Wales had a career-forming effect on her. She realised that 'expressing creativity is a part of mental health', that the shared activity of her studio had 'magic moments' of empathy, that art meant 'creating a [therapeutic] dialogue with yourself'.

She was (is) a socially-engaged artist but not an art therapist, so she decided early on to invite patients for three days a week to attempt any art they wanted to in her studio; some days five or six came along, other days fewer. One old lady, clearly institutionalised, painted the same picture every time she came. This consisted of rows of squares with coloured dots inside; she was purposeful and unvarying. Tessa encouraged self-confidence by putting on an arts festival at the Mid Wales when patients were encouraged to 'do their own thing' and then an exhibition of patients' work at the Wyeside Arts Centre in Builth Wells. For a time she was joined by a group of two dancers and a musician called 'Conscious Opera' who took over another empty ward, and taught expressive dance with long-stay patients. They put on a performance of dance pieces for the hospital which Tessa found 'very moving'.

Much as she enjoyed her work, Tessa was aware of a sense of anxiety that the hospital was running down. One nurse could not bear to visit E6 because the empty ward gave her a sense of loss. Then, the pace of decommissioning increased.

Zero

The School of Nursing was transferred to Swansea in 1992. Some long-stay and EMI wards remained. Above all, the admissions and acute services on Wards 7 and 8, where the specialized mental health treatment was based, continued as strong as ever. The Mid Wales was the only provider of such hospital services in Powys – surely this was case enough for survival?

Then in December 1994 Powys Health Authority published a devastating document: *The Promotion of Changes in Mental Health: Services leading to the closure of Mid Wales Hospital*. At this time all 48 beds on Wards 7 and 8 were occupied with patients who were 'acutely mentally ill' and there were still 97 patients in other wards suffering from 'psychiatry of old age.' But the recommendation was unequivocal:

> Powys Health Authority is of the view that a new unit for acute mental illness inpatients should be constructed in order to close Mid Wales hospital.
>
> The preferred option is that acute mental illness inpatient services should be provided for south Powys, i.e. Brecknock and Radnor, at Bronllys hospital. It is estimated that this would provide 25 beds…
>
> Acute mental illness inpatient services for north Powys should be provided in the proposed new hospital at Newtown. This unit would provide 15 beds.

It continued:

> The Health Authority no longer wishes mental illness inpatient services to be provided in old accommodation in mental illness hospitals. In addition, Powys Health Authority has established a standard that acute mental illness inpatient services should be provided within 40 minutes' travel time

for 80 per cent of the population served. [Therefore] the Health Authority does not intend to continue to purchase acute mental illness inpatient services from Mid Wales Hospital.

In other words, Michael Hession had got it right. Although a campaigner for the Mid Wales he had written a paper in the early 1990s:

The Mid Wales will always remain a rather forbidding institution based on nineteenth-century concepts of mental illness and treatment. In an area now with negligible public transport, the hospital is far removed from the centres of population and numerous demands will be made on the Health Authority's hospital transport service if the Mid Wales hospital is to provide the kind of hospital service appropriate to the next century.

Being remote from its population the hospital is difficult for communities [outside Talgarth] to identify with and the fears and prejudices about old-style asylums will, to some extent, be perpetuated.

Michael Hession retired in 1996. Delcie Davies had retired in 1990. After her retirement she was asked in 1992 by Powys Health Authority to chair a committee to choose between the Mid Wales and Bronllys. Her committee chose the Mid Wales:

I produced a report after a lot of hard work recommending that we keep the Mid Wales hospital, close Bronllys, convert 7s and 8s, the admission wards, into wards for Bronllys hospital so they would still be a bit separate. All the people working at the Mansion House [at Bronllys where the Powys Health Authority was based at that time] could be accommodated on the male side of the wards that were vacated, keeping the other side for psychiatric patients…

I know for a fact that Powys Health Authority favoured our proposal but they decided they would pay £75,000 for outside consultants [to get their view].

Coopers Lybrand reported that Bronllys was the 'best' option, presumably for reasons given in the 1994 *Promotion of Changes* paper quoted from earlier and anticipated by Michael Hession. It said that the Mid Wales was too isolated and the accommodation too 'old mental illness hospital' (meaning it was a former asylum but that was a taboo word). There was a strong practical reason too. There was spare capacity at Bronllys. Its original function as a TB sanatorium for South Wales miners suffering from emphysema had ended with the closure of the mines a decade or so earlier. More recently, beds had become available at Bronllys as a result of learning disability patients being resettled into the community. Now the beds could be taken up by the EMIs (Elderly Mentally Ill) still remaining at the Mid Wales. Nonetheless, other rumours about the decision went around Talgarth such as that the Local Health Authority was too lazy to move its headquarters from Bronllys. To add salt to the wound, the £4 million budget for the Mid Wales (less £1m that went towards the Health Authority's financial deficit) had to fund the whole re-provision programme, not just the new unit at Bronllys that cost £220,000.

Phil Pashley has a unique view comparing the Mid Wales Hospital with Bronllys because he was a patient at the former and taught poetry at the latter. He much preferred the Mid Wales. The location was beautiful, he says, and the atmosphere was more informal. He particularly liked the annexes next to the wards where patients could make snacks and sit around chatting.

In 1990 Keith Parry had become the last Manager of the Mid Wales Hospital and in 1992 he combined the job with managing Bronllys Hospital as well, so he oversaw the commissioning of services to the new site. Hitherto he had been seconded from the Mid Wales to the new Powys Health Care NHS Trust to prepare a business plan for the closure of the Mid Wales so he was prepared for the fraught time ahead. His job was to manage 'natural wastage', hasten the transfer of remaining patients to community care and oversee the building of the new acute ward at Bronllys. How did he react to opposition from the staff at the Mid Wales?

Staff resistance, yeah! There was clearly some resistance, particularly from the older staff, for whom I have the greatest respect. You see, there wasn't a family in Talgarth who didn't have members working at the hospital. The changes were threatening the workforce and this anxiety was transferred to the patients. But there's no doubt in my mind that it was the right thing to do. The pace was gradual and managed, unlike what happened to decommissioning [of former asylums] in the inner cities.

I had a good team working for me, particularly my senior nurse, Tina Morris, and she had an extremely good relationship with the nursing staff.

Many patients saw a better quality of life after they moved out and I can say that from an informed position because after closure I worked for the Brecon and District Contact Association, now MIND [the mental health charity], and I saw many ex-patients living in the community, some as volunteers, some getting jobs and having relationships and doing all sorts of interesting things. I saw very few sitting on park benches.

If you look at the whole process with a balanced perspective, and I've tried to, and bear in mind I've lived here all my life, OK?, I was the hospital manager who had to manage the process but I've no doubt it was the right thing to do. And I'm trying to give you that without any bias.

He added later that none of the Mid Wales staff lost jobs. Either they retired or moved to Bronllys Hospital, or into the community care services. Last out was Charge Nurse Brian Evans, who in April 2000 moved the very frail EMIs to M ward at Bronllys, where they remained until they died. He was one of those who thought the decommissioning was well-managed but he didn't think it was necessary. Community care was not working, he said, and he would have kept the Mid Wales open even if the name was changed to break the connection with its history.

On 4 March 2000, a *Thanksgiving Service and Concert to Mark the Closure of the Hospital* was held at the Mid Wales. Keith Parry pronounced the epitaph:

> The staff and all associated with the hospital, over the years, without doubt, sometimes in very difficult circumstances, provided services appropriate to the time. In so doing, we are now adjusting and responding to the ever-changing challenges of health care.
>
> It is the end of an era and therefore we must move on.

Moving on has not been easy. Writing soon after closure about the impact on the town of Talgarth, Patrick Sharman was in a black mood:

> Shops have closed, pubs barely tick over [three have actually closed], the population has ceased to expand and the primary school figures are at an all-time low. The fabric of the town has become jaded, with townspeople showing little interest in the future.
>
> With the hospital we shared a communal 'thing'. People of Talgarth felt a sense of loyalty and pride to both. Now people in the town do not appear to have a sense of belonging or ownership.

An aerial view of the Mid Wales in 2005

Nearly two decades later Talgarth appears to have recovered its spirit. 'Foreigners' have moved in who have revived the economy, at least. Former staff of the Mid Wales appear to look back with nostalgia and pride and little bitterness about the last years.

But what about that ghastly, vandalized, semi-ruined building 'up top' where for a century stood one of the most impressive institutions in mid-Wales? Walking round it today, Enoch Powell's description half a century ago always comes to mind.

> There they stand, isolated, majestic, imperious, brooded over by the gigantic water-tower and chimney combined, rising unmistakable and daunting out of the countryside – the asylums which our forefathers built with such immense solidity to express the notions of their day.

Powell then spoke to the future as though he were advising CADW (the Welsh Government service to protect historic buildings) in 2000:

> The very idea of these monuments derelict or demolished arouses an instinctive resistance in the mind. Well, let me declare that if we err, it is our duty to err on the side of ruthlessness. For the great majority of these establishments there is no appropriate future use, and I for my own part will resist any attempt to foist another purpose upon them.

Perhaps it would have been better in 2000 to have cleared the site and begun to build again for whatever purpose. However, I challenge the phrase 'no appropriate future use' referring to the time when Powell wrote the speech in 1961. What I think after two to three years writing this book is that for the last half-century of its existence, as for the first half century, the Mid Wales changed with the times and always did its best to care for the mentally ill when society had little else to offer. It was a total institution wherein staff and patients lived their lives according to the aphorism of the philosopher Bertrand Russell: 'Real life is a perpetual compromise between the ideal and the possible'.

Frank Bangay was a patient in Springfield mental hospital, formerly an asylum, in the 1970s. Now it is the headquarters of the South West London and St George's Mental Health NHS Trust, but in the 1990s there was talk of converting it into luxury flats, as indeed there was at the Mid Wales. Frank wrote this poem in 2004. If you believe in ghosts and are walking around the site of the Mid Wales you may see and hear these shuffling feet.

Those shuffling feet from the past

What nice grounds the Victorians gave the insane,
The Funny Farm (suitable for labour);
then came industrial therapy,
putting things in boxes, putting things in boxes,
putting things in boxes, putting things in boxes –
a few bob at the end of the week, twenty cigarettes;
well it keeps the mind active, or so it was said.

The water tower it winked at me;
the years of struggle that beat the spirit down,
Those shuffling feet just keep on walking...
an endless road along psychiatric corridors.

Our songs will rise, our songs will rise,
breaking through the walls of discrimination.
Our songs will rise, our songs will rise,
tearing down the walls of exploitation.

Such spacious grounds the Victorians gave the insane:
the trees still blossom and the birds still sing.

Cries from the past, hear them echo;
shuffling feet on hospital lino.
Keep on walking, smoke another cigarette,
cigarette smoke coming through the air vents.
Admissions,
Sections,
Acute Ward,
Long-stay Ward –
Now they can rent or buy a home here,
mind you, never set up home in the ECT Room.

On medication we feel drowsy,
on medication we pace up and down.
Those shuffling feet just keep on walking…
an endless road along psychiatric corridors.
So as you walk round this property developers' dream,
walk alongside those shuffling feet from the past;
those institutionalised clothes
never became a fashion item
But our daily struggles can lead to nervous breakdowns.

And as you walk around the grounds, around the grounds,
around the grounds, if someone comes up to you and says
'Got a fag? Got 10p?'
don't be alarmed, don't be alarmed,
they're just trying to communicate,
they're just trying to be your friend.

Acknowledgements

I am very grateful to all the staff who allowed me to interview them, sometimes more than once, over the last two years. They are, in alphabetical order: Vernon Argent, Ken and Janet Bowen, Delcie Davies, Bill and Sylvia Devereux, Brian and Joan Devereux, Malcolm Dodds, Brian Evans, Annie, Jill and Judy Fawke, Monty Graham MBE, Donald Harris, Dr Michael Hession, David Lewis, Phil Luffman, Gerald McArthey, Bill Morgan, Keith Parry, Andrew Price, Patrick Sharman and Tessa Waite.

I am also grateful to three former patients: Jonathan Morgan, who allowed me to interview him and quote from his book, Phil Pashley for his poetry and Tom Hampshire, who has lent me some of his photos: also to two contributors who wished to remain anonymous.

Thanks also to the Talgarth History Society, two of whose members, Virginia Brown and Jill Fawke, have given me particular help.

My thanks also to Phil Collins, the present owner of the site, for allowing me to look round it; Gaynor Davis, for reminding me about the Mad Woman of *Kilvert's Diary*; Sue Morgan, daughter of Jean Morgan MBE, for providing me with her mother's photo; Peter Williams of the *Brecon and Radnor Express* for the photo on the back cover, Jacqueline Morgan of Brecon Museum for providing photos, and Roy Thomas, a local farmer, for remembering the POW experience on his farm.

I formally acknowledge that the photos of patients used in the first chapter are 'By permission of Powys County Archive'. I sincerely thank Powys County Archive and the Collections and Research Archive at the Wellcome Library; also the Public Records Office at Kew. The photograph on page 102 is 'By permission of the Museum of History and Industry (MOHAI)', Seattle, and that on page 105 is 'By permission of Getty Images'.

I have found the following books most helpful:

Bedlam, the Asylum and Beyond, The Wellcome Collection (Thames & Hudson, 2016)

Our Voices, the audio companion to *Bedlam,* from which *Those shuffling feet from the past* by Frank Bangay is taken

Roy Porter, *Madness, a Brief History* (OUP, 2002)

Christopher Frith and Eve Johnstone, *Schizophrenia, a Very Short Introduction* (OUP, 2003)

Mark Stevens, *Life in the Victorian Asylum* (Pen and Sword, 2014)

Mark Davis, *Asylum, Inside the Pauper Lunatic Asylums* (Amberley, 2014)

Peter Leese, *Shell Shock* (Macmillan, 2014)

Edgar Jones and Simon Wessely, *Shell Shock to PTSD, Military Psychiatry from 1900 to the Gulf War* (Psychology Press, 2014)

Jon and Diane Sutherland, *Prisoner of War Camps in Britain* (Golden Guides Press, 2012)

Miriam Kochan, *Prisoners of England* (Macmillan, 1980), from which the poem *Lament and Letters* by Egon Schormann are taken.

Stephen McGinty, *Camp Z* (Quercus, 2011)

Jonathan Morgan, *The Tragedy of War: Essays on the Welsh War Poets, Artists and Writers and Those in the Welsh Regiments* (2014)

I hope those who know the Mid Wales hospital better than I do find my book fair. It is certainly intended to be. I hope those who are interested in the subject of mental illness do not find my book sensationalist or vicariously shocking. It is not intended to be. I emerge from two years' research wiser and possibly sadder than before.

Index

Argent, Vernon	173, 175
Ashley, April…'Queen of Hay'	151
Bangay, Frank	191-193
Barnes, Mary… artist	171-2
Bhakta, Dr Mohan	137, 144, 157, 161, 164
Board of Control	49-50, 63-4
Boarding Out Officer	54
Bowen, Ken and Janet	154-6
Brecknock and Radnor Joint Asylum	8, 13, 15, 20, 28, 32
Admissions	21, 47, 51
Casualty Report Book 1911	37
Census of 1911	19, 34
Change of name, 1921	52
Chapel	17, 56, 159
Daily routine	45
Discharges and Deaths	21, 28-33
Epileptic cases	16, 33, 37, 51
General Rules for Attendants and Nurses 1904-5	34-43, 45-6
Nightingale wards	17, 139
Opening day	8, 13-4, 19
Patients' funding	19-22
Religious mania	29
Self-sufficiency	19, 46, 130, 178
Shell-shock, WW1	49-52
Suicides	41-2
Syphilis	32
Brecon County Times	12, 15, 34, 42, 44
Brecon & Radnor Gazette	122
Buchthal, Arnold alias White	86-7

CADW 190

Chemical revolution 112-114

    Antabus 167, 170

    Cardiazol 77

    Chloral hydrate 47, 80

    Largactil 112-4, 161

    Lythium salts 47

    Paraldehyde 47, 80, 113-4

    Sparine 112

    Stelazine 161

Chipchase, Matron 17, 34-5

Commissioners in Lunacy 20-1, 45, 49

Davies, Delcie 25, 95-8, 137, 155, 173, 180-2, 186

Davies, Gaynor 7-9

Davies, Gladys 26, 113, 125

Deep sleep therapy 110-11

Devereux, Bill 59, 78, 89, 106, 114, 120, 124, 130, 142, 182

Devereux, Brian 97, 107, 114, 153

Devereux, Joan 107, 112-4, 121-123, 141-2, 146-7, 153

Devereux, Sylvia 123, 183

Diggle, Dr Gordon 25, 47-8, 93-4, 96-8, 108, 121, 125-8, 137

Directorate of Army Psychiatry 62-3, 67

Dodds, Malcolm 175-6

Drug therapy (see Chemical revolution)

Drummond (Lt Col.), Peter 49, 53-4, 62, 64-6, 69, 76-82, 87, 90, 92

Electroconvulsive therapy/ECT 76, 80, 98, 101, 103-111

Evans, Brian 148, 189

Fallowell, Duncan 151

Fawke, Albert 24-5, 49

Fawke, Jill 86

Fawke, Judy 89

Fenlon, Mary 164, 173, 175

Freeman, Dr Walter (USA) 100-102
General Nursing Council(GNC) 92-93, 110, 118, 124-6, 129, 135-6, 138
Glanusk, Lord 8, 35, 49, 56
Graham, Monty 93, 131, 144, 164, 180
Hand, Dr 121, 126
Harris, Donald 155, 162, 165-8
Hess, Deputy Führer Rudolph 82-87
Hession, Dr Michael 26, 77, 102, 109, 112, 137, 143-144, 152, 157-160, 162, 164, 169-171, 174, 180-182, 186-187
Institutionalisation 16, 116, 138-143, 165
Jones, Dr Ernest W 34, 47
Kilvert, Rev. Francis 7, 20
Laing, R D 171-2
Lawrence, Matron 67
Leucotomy 98-103
Lewis, David 110-1, 138, 180
Lewis, Gwyn 119, 137
Limentani, Major Amedeo (Adam) 77
Lobotomy (see Leucotomy)
Luffman, Phil 162, 171-2
Lunatic Asylums Act, 1845 and 1890 20, 23
'Mad Valley' 24
McCarthy, Gerald 108, 138, 140, 144, 147, 173
McKissock, Mr Wylie 98-102
Mawr, Matron Mary 97, 109, 120, 122-3, 129, 168, 173
Mental Deficiency Act 1913 23, 25, 27
Mental Treatment Act 1915 51
Mental Treatment Act 1930 54
Mental Health Acts 1959 and 1983 26, 104, 126-7, 138, 143
Mental Health Resource Centres 137-8, 180
Mental Health Tribunal 143-4

Mid Wales Hospital, The   8-11
   Admissions wards 7 and 8   156-63, 169-70, 185
   Alcoholism, treatment   167, 169
   Bathing Rules   48
   Behavioural therapy   164-8
   Coopers Lybrand report   187
   Community psychiatric nurses introduced   138
   Education Centre for junior doctors and GPs   174
   Horticultural Show, Sports and fetes   144-5
   Mother and Baby unit   171
   Name change 1961   132
   Outpatient clinics   126, 137-8, 164
   Pallbearers   110, 155
   Patients' Advocate   152
   Patients' Council   152
   Patient outings and social life   153-155
   Powys School of Nursing   128, 175, 176
   Psychotherapy   169-70
   Register of deaths and burials   55
   Suicide Caution Card   41-2
   Tegfan   118, 120, 164, 166, 169, 181
   Welfare of Staff   92-3
   Welsh-speakers   52
Mid Wales Mental Hospital: name changes, 1921 and 1961   52, 132
MIND   188
Morgan, Ken   39, 41
Morgan, Jean   158-9, 162
Morgan, Jonathan   159, 161
Morris, Tina   188
Mortuary   16, 110, 155-6
National Health Services Act 1948   10, 93
Nuremburg War Trials   86, 87

Occupational therapy   46, 67, 92, 116, 124-5, 128, 124-5, 140, 148-9, 164, 172-3

Parry, Keith   115-8, 144, 147, 152-3, 173, 187-9

Pashley, Phil   163, 182, 187

Phillips, Dr Alan   137

Poor Law Union   20, 22, 26

Powell, Enoch   8, 132-4, 136, 190

Powys Health Authority   136, 180-1, 185-7

Powys Health Care NHS Trust   188

Promotion of Changes in Mental Health: Leading to the Closure of the Mid Wales Hospital   185

Price, Andrew   53

Pugh, Dr Robert   34, 49, 53

RAF Association, Talgarth   90

Rast, Dr Hugo, diaries   11, 70, 73, 75-79, 82

Sharman, Patrick   145, 148-9, 161, 177-8, 182, 189

Shirley, Dame Stephanie   86

South Wales Sanatorium/Bronllys Hospital   48, 53, 177, 180, 185-189

Spanish Civil War, the case of Serefino M   87-88

Talgarth Military Hospital, for allied servicemen and women   59-69

    Camp 234 for Prisoners of War   59-60, 69-82

    Commonwealth War Graves Commission   88

    Pioneer Corps   32, 37, 44-45

    Queen Alexandra's Imperial Military Nursing Service   33

    Royal Army Medical Corps   31, 33

    Shell shock, WW2   59-60, 62, 68,89-90

    Staff working hours   67

    Suicides   70, 78, 84, 92

    War Diary of Lt Col. Drummond   64-66, 69, 78, 82

Talgarth: impact of closure; and recovery   189-90

Visiting Committee   21, 23-25, 27, 32, 35-36, 43-4, 46, 49-51, 53-55, 63-64, 67, 69, 87, 98, 119, 124-6

Waite, Tessa… Artist in Residence 1990 — 183
War Office — 62, 67, 69, 75, 79, 84
   Mixed Medical Commission (MMC) — 70, 73, 75, 79, 85
Weale, Arnold — 116-7, 152, 174
Welsh Border Hospital Management Committee — 52, 93, 108, 118
Welsh Office, The — 138
Williams, Gwyn — 59
Workhouses — 20-23, 27, 54

Up Top is just one of a whole range of
publications from Y Lolfa. For a full
list of books currently in print, send now
for your free copy of our new full-colour
catalogue. Or simply surf into our website

www.ylolfa.com

for secure on-line ordering.

TALYBONT CEREDIGION CYMRU SY24 5HE
e-mail ylolfa@ylolfa.com
website www.ylolfa.com
phone (01970) 832 304
fax 832 782

Ask for a print quote!
01970 832 304